RUNNING OS/2

RUNNING
OS/2

Michael I. Hyman

BANTAM BOOKS

TORONTO • NEW YORK • LONDON • SYDNEY • AUCKLAND

To my grandparents . . . .

RUNNING OS/2
A Bantam Book / February 1988

ISBN 0-553-34566-4

Published simultaneously in the United States and Canada

Bantam Books are published by Bantam Books, Inc. Its trademark, consisting of the
words "Bantam Books" and the portrayal of a rooster, is Registered in U.S. Patent
and Trademark Office and in other countries. Marca Registrada, Bantam Books,
Inc., 666 Fifth Avenue, New York, New York 10103.

PRINTED IN THE UNITED STATES OF AMERICA

0   9   8   7   6   5   4   3   2

Acknowledgements

I would especially like to thank Bill Gates and Steve Ballmer of Microsoft; Pete Maruhnic, Terry Lucas, and Joe Venuto of October Associates; Rainer McCown of Rhinetek; Dr. Daniel Bakal, Barbara Greene, Michael Bakal, and William Van Besien; and, of course, Richard, Roberta, and Betsy Hyman.

Contents

C H A P T E R   1

Introduction to OS/2   1

CHAPTER 4

The Basics

CHAPTER 5

Installing Applications

Introduction

OS/2 is an exciting new operating system for Intel 80286- and 80386-based personal computers. In many respects, OS/2 is quite similar to DOS, yet in other ways it is much more powerful and complicated. In addition, just as there are differences between PC-DOS and MS-DOS, there will also be differences between OS/2 designed for the IBM (IBM OS/2) and OS/2 designed for other 80286 and 80386 personal computers (MS OS/2). This book will teach you the fundamentals of using OS/2 and the differences between DOS, IBM OS/2, and MS OS/2.

You'll start by learning the overall features of OS/2 and operating systems in general. Then, you'll learn about disk organization, files, and devices and about some important OS/2 commands — critical information for computer users.

This is followed by the chapter on how to use the Session Manager — the OS/2 control program. This unique program will be a central part of all your OS/2 work sessions. You'll also learn about entering OS/2 commands, getting help if you have problems, and installing applications.

The next section of the book contains an in-depth alphabetical list of all of the OS/2 commands, with examples of their uses. Special differences between DOS and OS/2 are noted. This is followed by a special chapter offering power tips on getting the most out of OS/2 commands.

The next few chapters cover piping, redirecting, grouping, creating batch files, and customizing OS/2 through start-up batch programs and configuration files. This section also includes information on installing and using device drivers.

Next comes a chapter on installing OS/2 and a chapter containing powerful utility programs that you can type in and use. The last chapter contains a quick summary of the most important OS/2 commands.

How to Use This Book

Users are urged to read the book through. Don't worry if some ideas seem foreign or complicated. As you read on and work with OS/2, you'll become more and more comfortable with the material. Try to become familiar with as many of the OS/2 commands as possible. You'll find the most important commands — the ones you'll need to memorize — in Appendix A.

For those of you who are familiar with MS-DOS or PC-DOS, differences between OS/2 and DOS are specially indicated.

1

Introduction to OS/2

OS/2 is a powerful new operating system for personal computers. It incorporates important features previously found only on minicomputers and mainframes. This chapter reviews OS/2's basic features.

Multitasking

OS/2 is a *multitasking* operating system.[1] This means that you can run several applications at the same time. For example, you can manipulate data in a spreadsheet while an accounting program is calculating your month-end accounts and is printing payroll checks. At the same time, your desktop publishing package could be formatting a newsletter.

Multitasking is very useful because you don't have to put off working on one project until the computer finishes work-

---

[1] Technically speaking, it is a prioritized time-sliced multitasking system. Every few milliseconds OS/2 switches between tasks. Tasks with higher priority will get more processor time.

ing on another. You can also switch between applications without having to save and return to work in progress.

With OS/2, not only can more than one program run at once, but each program can have sections that run in parallel. This is a very powerful feature for software developers.

Memory

With OS/2, each program can use up to 16 megabytes (M) of memory — that's 16,777,216 bytes. This is 25 times as much memory as old DOS applications could use. Even if your machine doesn't have that much memory in RAM, you can still access huge amounts because OS/2 uses *virtual memory*. This means that if OS/2 needs more memory than you have in RAM, it will temporarily use disk space for memory.[2]

Being able to access large amounts of memory opens up a myriad of new possibilities for PC programs. Large memory access is crucial for many business and scientific applications that previously could not be done on personal computers.

Protected Mode

With DOS, memory is broken up into several sections. DOS uses certain sections of memory to store crucial information; programs use other sections of memory. If memory-resident utilities are loaded, several programs are active at the same time, each using its own sections of memory. But, any program can access the memory of any other. If one of these programs has a mistake, it can overrun memory, causing it to crash — and more importantly, causing all of the other programs, including DOS, to crash.

[2] With virtual memory, programs do not reference machine memory addresses. All memory addresses, such as those returned by a malloc call, are relative to the particular program. OS/2 converts these relative addresses to a machine-specific address. The machine-specific address can change throughout operation, as memory is moved around or paged to disk.

With OS/2, several programs can run at once, but programs can't look at the memory of other programs. In fact, programs never even know if other programs are running. As far as they can tell, they have control over all of the system's resources.

Protected mode[3] is very important for multitasking operating systems. It ensures that if one program crashes, other programs can work without interruption. With protected mode and virtual memory a program can be designed as though it is the only one that will run. This makes work much easier for software developers.

Presentation Manager

The Presentation Manager is another exciting feature of OS/2. It is a windowing graphical user interface, much like Microsoft Windows. The user can select commands, start up programs, and access disk files by simply pointing with a mouse. Several programs can appear on the screen at once, each in its own movable window. Presentation Manager programs are almost intuitive to learn. It is also easy to transfer data back and forth between programs.

Compatibility Mode

Because so many users already have DOS programs, OS/2 has a *compatibility mode* that lets it run DOS programs. This saves users from buying and learning new programs. Because some software companies (especially those out of business) won't transfer their DOS programs to OS/2, old software packages can still be run. This is a very nice feature. Some programs, however, such as memory-resident utilities, won't be able to run in OS/2's compatibility mode.

[3] Protected mode is a specific operational feature of the 80286 and 80386 chips. The chips maintain a look up table for each task mapping virtual address space to physical address space. Tasks cannot access memory assigned to other tasks.

OS/2 System Requirements

OS/2 is a very sophisticated operating system, and it requires a sophisticated computer to support it. In order to run OS/2, you must have an 80286- or 80386- based computer, such as an IBM AT, Compaq 386, or PS/2 50. The computer must have a hard disk, at least one floppy drive, and as much memory as possible. While you can run OS/2 with 640K of memory, you need 1 or 2M of RAM to take full advantage of its features. Since memory is very inexpensive, try to put at least 2 to 4M in your computer.

Summary

- OS/2 is multitasking. Several programs can run simultaneously.
- OS/2 can address up to 16M of memory per application. This is accomplished through virtual memory addressing.
- Because OS/2 operates in protected mode, programs cannot access other programs' memory.
- Presentation Manager programs have an easy-to-use windowed graphical interface.
- Old DOS applications can run in OS/2's compatibility mode.
- OS/2 needs an 80286- or 80386-based computer with a hard disk, a floppy drive, and lots of RAM.

C H A P T E R

2

What Operating Systems Do

In this chapter you'll learn about the basic function of operating systems and the types of hardware they deal with. You'll also learn about the environment and partitions.

Operating Systems

The *operating system* is the hub of the computer. It provides a bridge between the user, programs, and the computer's hardware. The operating system controls the interaction between the user and the peripherals. For example, the operating system supervises files, printers, and the screen display.

The operating system works at three levels — between the user and programs, between programs and the hardware, and between the computer and peripherals.

For example, when you type in a command to start a program or copy a file, you are interacting with the operating system. The operating system converts your request to a series of very complicated machine instructions that you are fortunately unaware of.

If you are running your word processor and decide to save a file, the program sends a request to the operating system. The operating system then acts on this command, converting it to a complicated series of instructions.

Because the operating system handles all the low-level "nitty-gritty" interaction with the hardware, users and programmers can be much more productive.

Peripherals

There are several common *peripherals* — computer devices — with which the operating system interacts. These include the screen, keyboard, mouse, printers, and disk drives.

There are many different types of computer screens. Some allow only text characters, while others allow black and white or color graphics. Some color graphics screens display up to four colors at once; others display several million colors at once.

The keyboard is the basic way in which people interact with the computer. You enter commands and data from the keyboard. While there are several different styles of keyboards, they all perform the same function.

Mice are another way of entering commands and data. They let the user move a cursor to point to an item or push a button to select a command. Mice vary in the number and location of their buttons. Some mice are based on optical operation, and some on mechanical operation.

Printers and plotters are the way that information is passed from the computer to other people. Printers and plotters transfer data from the computer to paper (or acetate). There are many different kinds of printers: thermal, dot matrix, daisy wheel, ink jet, laser, and so forth. There are also several types of plotters. Both devices come in different sizes and speeds.

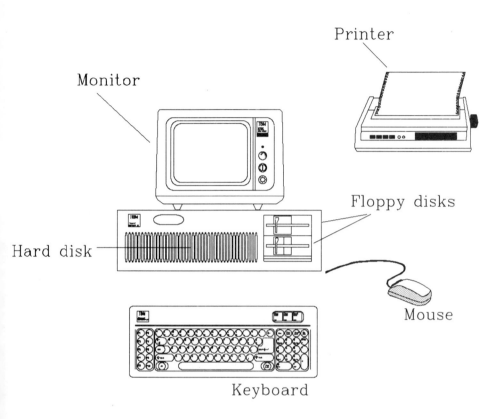

Figure 2-1 Microcomputer peripherals — Printer, floppy disks, mouse, keyboard, hard disk, and monitor.

Disks are used to store information. Disks can remember information even when the computer is turned off. There are two main types of disks: floppy disks and hard disks. Floppy disks hold less information than hard disks, but they are easily transferred from machine to machine. For example, when you buy a program, it comes to you on a floppy. In general, floppy disks hold from 160K to 2M of data. Hard disks hold a lot more information and are faster, but they generally stay put in one computer. Hard disks are used for storing programs and information that you will access over and over again. Hard disks can store from 10M to several hundred megabytes of data.

Summary

- The operating system is a bridge between the user, programs, and the hardware.
- Most computers have peripherals such as a screen, keyboard, mouse, printer, and disk drive.

C H A P T E R

3

Disk Organization

All programs and data are stored on disks. Disks should be organized so that data can be found and used easily. In this chapter you'll learn about disks, files, and directories.

Disks

There are several different types of floppy disks. Each holds different amounts of memory. The early PC's use *double-sided double-density* disks, abbreviated *DS/DD*. These disks are 5 1/4 inches square and can hold up to 360K of information. ATs can use *high-density 5 1/4-inch* disks. These disks can hold up to 1.2M of memory. Many laptop computers use *low-density 3 1/2-inch* disks. These disks are 3 1/2 inches square and can hold up to 720K of information. PS/2's use *high-density 3 1/2-inch* disks, which can hold up to 1.44M of information.

Another type of disk is the *hard disk*. Unlike floppy disks, hard disks aren't removable. The same hard disk always stays inside the computer. Hard disks can store and retrieve information much faster than floppy disks. They also store much more information than floppy disks. Hard disks for the early XTs stored 10M of information. Now, hard disks of 30M to over 100M are common.

A third type of disk is the *cartridge hard disk*. These are a combination of floppy disks and hard disks. They are removable disks that can store 10M or more each. Like hard disks, they are fast and hold a lot of data; like floppies, they can be transferred between machines, and many can be used, thus giving unlimited storage potential.

Disk Structure

When the operating system stores information on a disk, it needs to know how to find one datum out of all those on the disk. It can do so because of the way the disk is physically organized. While only advanced users ever access disks at this *low level*, beginning users should be familiar with the terms that describe the disk's low-level structure.

Disks are circular *platters* of electromagnetic material. They spin around very quickly inside the disk drive. A little electromagnet, called the *head*, moves back and forth over the disk, reading or writing information. Floppy disks have a top and bottom *side*. Hard disks have several sides — two for each platter.

Each side of the disk is broken into concentric rings of information called *tracks*. Each track is further broken into areas of information called *sectors*. Typically, there are 512 bytes within each sector. To read a byte from the disk, the disk drive moves the head to the track where the byte is located and then waits until the sector containing the byte rotates under the head. Then, it reads the whole sector and fishes out the byte.

Because there can be hundreds of thousands of sectors on a disk, OS/2 combines sectors into units called *clusters*. A

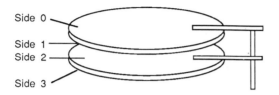

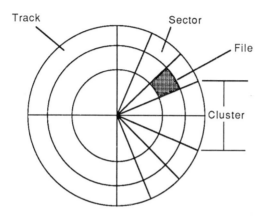

Figure 3-1 Disk's components — Sides, track sector, file, and cluster.

cluster is usually formed by one to eight sectors. Files are composed of groups of clusters (Figure 3.1).

Files

Files are the basic unit of storage on disks. You save and load all your information from files. A file can be a legal document, a spreadsheet, a database, or a term paper. Programs are also stored in files. For example, your word processor is a program file.

As you will see in Chapter 4, when you type the name of the file containing a program, the program runs. The program might ask you for the names of files containing data. When

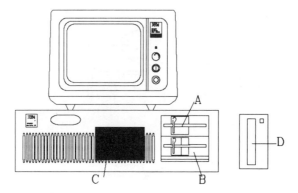

Figure 3-2 Drive names — Floppy drives A and B, internal hard disk drive C, and external hard disk drive D.

you supply them, the program will let you access the data in the files.

Disk Drive and File Names

Because a computer can have several disk drives, OS/2 has names for each drive. That way you can tell programs what drive contains the file you want to run or access. All disks drives are given single-letter names, such as A or C. The primary floppy drive is called the *A* drive. This is the floppy drive that whirs when you first turn on the machine. The first hard disk is called the *C* drive. If you have two floppies, the second is usually the *B* drive. If you have a second hard disk or a RAM disk, or an external drive, they will be called *D*, *E*, and so forth (Figure 3.2).

Files also have names. File names are up to 11 characters long. The first eight letters of a file name are separated from the last three by a period. These last three letters are called the file name *extension*. File names can contain a combination of any of the letters of the alphabet, the numbers, and the following special characters: ~ ! @ # $ % ' ' ( ) - { }

For example, here are some file names: ACCOUNTS.MPW, LOVELET.TXT, 4-15-70.RC, CONFIG.SYS, CC.EXE. As you can see, you don't need to use all 11 letters. You also don't need to have an extension. Here are some more file names: README, GREATFUN, 1COMPUTE. If you do use an extension, however, you must type a period before you type the extension.

To tell the computer what file to use, you tell it the drive and the file name. Separate the two by a colon. For example, to tell the computer to use the LOVELET.TXT file on the A drive, you would tell it A:LOVELET.TXT. To use the README file from the C drive, you would tell it C:README.

The file name extension is often used to describe what type of information is in the file. Here are some common file name extensions conventions:

Extension	Type of File
BAT	Batch file (a type of program)
CMD	Command file (a type of program)
COM	Program
DIF	Generic spreadsheet file
DLL	Dynamic link library (a special file for programmers)
DOC	Text file
EXE	Program
LIB	Library (a special file for programmers)
PLW	Spreadsheet file
PIC	Picture
SYS	System file (tells OS/2 information about the computer or a peripheral)
TXT	Text file
WKS	Spreadsheet file

Device Names

Incidentally, disk drives aren't the only peripherals with OS/2 names. The printer is called *PRN*, the keyboard and the screen are called *CON*, and the modem is called *COM1, COM2,* or *COM3*.

When to Use Hard Disks and Floppy Disks

Because your hard disk holds more information and accesses it faster than floppy disk drives, you should use it to hold your programs and most of your data. Use the floppy disks to make *backups* of the data and programs on your hard disk. Also use floppy disks for transferring files from one computer to another and for storing data files or programs that you rarely use. For example, you might want to store personal letters, copies of paid invoices, out-of-date tax information, or other such data on floppies. Your primary use of floppies will be to load new programs onto your hard disk.

Preparing Floppy Disks for Use

When you buy a box of floppy disks, they are usually *unformatted*. This means that they don't have the markings on them that OS/2 uses to find sectors. Before you can use a new floppy disk for storing information, you need to format it. To do this, you place the floppy disk in the A drive, and type:

```
FORMAT A: /V
```

The disk drive will start whirring. After a little, a message asking you for a volume name will appear. OS/2 will display this name whenever you list the names of the files on the disk. The volume name helps remind you which disk is in the drive. Type in a name of up to 11 characters. After you hit Return, OS/2 will ask you if you want to format another disk. Enter N for no. Take a blank label out of the disk box and write the name that you gave the disk on it. Peel the label off and put it on the disk — place it on the upper right corner of 5 1/4-inch disks and on the top of 3 1/2-inch disks.

Once you have formatted a disk, you can use it for saving files. You'll learn more about putting files on disks at the end of this chapter.

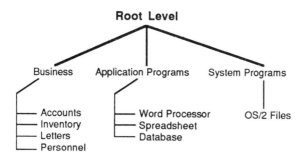

Figure 3-3 Directory structure.

Note: you only need to format a disk before its first use. After you have formatted it once, you don't need to format it again unless the disk becomes magnetically damaged, which is unlikely. Every time that you format it, all the data that was on it previously is erased.

Directories

Because disks can hold thousands of files, they are organized into a *directory* system. Each directory holds a related group of files. Instead of having to look through a list of thousands of names to find a file, you only need to look through a few names within a directory. For example, you could put all of your personal letters in a PERSONAL LETTER directory. Within this directory you could have another directory (a subdirectory) called MIRNA, for all of your letters to a person named Mirna.

Figure 3.3 shows such a directory system. Note that each directory is like a box. The box can hold several files and also other boxes. These boxes, in turn, can contain some files and more boxes.

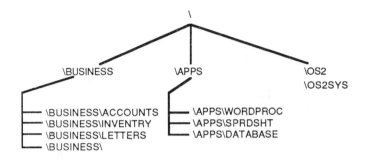

Figure 3-4 Directory system of Figure 3-3.

Directory Names

Like files, directories have names. Directory names are up to 11 characters long. You can use any name that you want, as long as it is composed of the letters, numbers, and the same special characters that file names can use. To make a directory name greater than eight characters long, you need to include a period before you type the last three letters, just as you do for typing file name extensions.

For example, Figure 3.4 shows the directory system of Figure 3.3 with OS/2 directory names.

The very top level directory is called the *root directory*. It is always named \. For example, the root directory on the C drive is *C:*. To specify a file that is located within a directory, you give the directory name followed by the file name. For example, the file CONFIG.SYS in the root directory of the A drive would be called *A:\CONFIG.SYS*. To indicate a directory within a directory, start with the root directory and list all directory names until you get to the last directory you want to access. Separate each directory name by a \. For example, to get to the file 1.LET in the subdirectory MIRNA, in the subdirectory LETTERS, in the directory PERSONAL, located in the root directory on the C drive, you would use *C:\PERSONAL\LETTERS\MIRNA\1.LET*. This says, go to the C drive, look in the root directory for the PERSONAL directory. Look in that directory for the LETTERS subdirectory. Look in that directory for the MIRNA subdirectory. In that directory, get the file 1.LET.

How to Organize Your Directory Structure

Plan your directory structure so that you can easily find the files that you need. Put all of the program files associated with a particular program in the same directory. For example, if your word processor has a spelling feature, put the dictionary in the same directory as the word processor. If several people will be using your computer, you might want to give each of them a directory. If you use the computer for business and home use, create business and personal directories. You can set up separate directories for key clients, purchase orders, overall accounting, or estimates. If you are a programmer, set up a language directory. Put in a separate directory for each of your compilers. For example, you could have directories called C, PASCAL, and PROLOG.

Think how to organize your directory before you begin to load applications and create data. It will save time as you use your disk. Some sample directory structures appear in Figure 3.5.

Examining a Disk's Directory Structure

You can see how your disk is organized using the TREE command. To use it, type:

```
TREE drive_name:
```

where *drive_name* is the name of the drive that you want to examine. For example, to see how the C disk is organized, type:

```
TREE C:
```

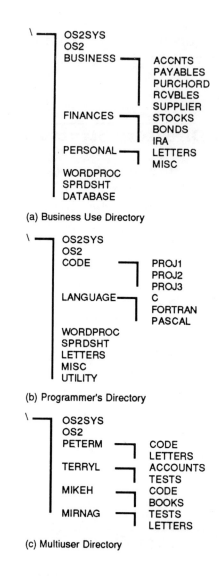

(a) Business Use Directory

(b) Programmer's Directory

(c) Multiuser Directory

Figure 3-5 Organizing your directory structure.

A listing of all your directories will appear on the screen as shown in Figure 3.6. If you want to make a print out of this structure, turn on your printer and type the following:

```
TREE C: > PRN
```

```
Directory path listing
Path: \DOS
Subdirectories:   None

Path: \UTILITY
Subdirectories:   None

Path: \OS2SYS
Subdirectories:   None

Path: \OS2
Subdirectories:   None

Path: \LANGUAGE
Subdirectories:   ASSM
                  BASIC
                  C
                  FORTRAN
                  PASCAL
                  PROLOG
                  TBC

  .
  .
  .
  .
```

Figure 3-6 Output from a TREE command.

This means, list the directory structure and send all the information to the printer. Note the use of the printer's name, PRN. The > symbol is the redirection symbol, to be discussed later.

Seeing What Files Are in a Directory

If you want to see what files are in a directory, use the DIR command. Its format is:

DIR *directory_name*

```
Volume in drive C is DISK1_VOL1
Directory of C:\

AUTOEXEC BAT        412   10-16-87    9:59a
CONFIG   SYS        350   10-14-87    8:09p
STARTUP  CMD        100   10-14-87    8:09p
OS2INIT  CMD        212   10-14-87    8:15p
DOS          <DIR>        10-14-87   11:13p
UTILITY      <DIR>        10-14-87   11:14p
OS2SYS       <DIR>        10-14-87   11:23p
OS2          <DIR>        10-14-87   11:24p
LANGUAGE     <DIR>        10-14-87   11:32p
TOOLS        <DIR>        10-14-87   11:26p
INCLUDE      <DIR>        10-14-87   11:27p
LIB          <DIR>        10-14-87   11:28p
INIT         <DIR>        10-14-87   11:28p
DEMOS        <DIR>        10-14-87   11:28p
SOURCES      <DIR>        10-14-87   11:30p
CONFIG       <DIR>        10-14-87   11:36p
WP           <DIR>        10-14-87   11:36p
WINDOWS      <DIR>        10-14-87   11:39p

     18 File(s)      9691136 bytes free
```

Figure 3-7 Sample output of DIR.

where *directory_name* is the name of the directory you want to examine. For example, if you wanted to see all the files in the root directory of the C drive, you would type:

```
DIR C:\
```

If you wanted to see all the files in the LANGUAGE directory of the C drive, you would type:

```
DIR C:\LANGUAGE
```

Note that the DIR command lists files and directories. It also tells the time and date that a file or directory was created and the size of files (Figure 3-7).

```
DIRECTORY PATH LISTING FOR VOLUME DISK1_VOL1

Files:            AUTOEXEC.BAT
                  CONFIG  .SYS
                  STARTUP .CMD
                  OS2INIT .CMD

Path: \DOS

Sub-directories:  None

Files:            ASSIGN  .COM
                  BACKUP  .COM
                  BASICA  .COM
                  CHKDSK  .COM
                  COMP    .COM

    .
    .
    .
```

Figure 3-8 Sample output of TREE C:IF.

Making a List of All Files on the Disk

If you want, you can make a list of all the files that are on the disk. To do so, type:

```
TREE drive_name: /F
```

For example, to get a list of all the files on the C drive, you would type:

```
TREE C: /F
```

A sample output appears in Figure 3.8.

Using Wild Cards with File Names

When you used the DIR command, you got a list of all the files in a directory. Sometimes you only want to see files that start with certain letters or that have a certain extension. To do so, you can use a file name template. OS/2 will only list files that match the template. For example, if you type:

```
DIR FOUR
```

OS/2 will list all files that have the first name FOUR and any extension. It might list FOUR.EXE, FOUR.WKS, and FOUR.BAT. Or, there might not be any files listed.

Adding *wild cards* lets you list a much broader range of files. Wild cards are symbols that tell OS/2 to match any letter in their position. The wild card *?* means match any character, and the wild card *means match any series of characters. For example, suppose the files in the TEST directory are:

```
FOUR
FOUR.EXE
FEAR
BEAR.COM
BEER.CAN
```

If you typed DIR C:\TEST\F??R, OS/2 would respond with FOUR, FOUR.EXE, and FEAR because all of these file names start with F, end with R, and have two characters in between. If you typed DIR C:\TEST\?E?R, you would see the files FEAR, BEAR.COM, and BEER.CAN listed. You can also use wild cards for the extension. For example, DIR C:\TEST\B*.C?? would cause BEAR.COM and BEER.CAN to be listed. You would get the same results from DIR C:\TEST\B*.C*.

If you want to list files with names satisfying several criteria, you can give **DIR** a list of name templates. For example, if you want to list file names that start with FE or have a COM extension, you can type:

```
DIR C:\TEST\FE* C:\TEST\*.COM
```

Using wild cards is a very powerful technique. It lets you specify a group of files without having to list each individually. This is extremely useful for finding files with particular contents. For example, if all of your letters to Bob had names starting with BOB, DIR BOB* would list all of your letters to Bob. Likewise, you can find all of your spreadsheet files by looking for the spreadsheet file extension. Wild cards are also very useful when you are copying and erasing files.

The Default Drive and Directory

Most of the time you will be working with files in a particular drive. You do not need to constantly specify the drive name when referring to those files. Instead, you can leave out a drive name, and OS/2 will use the *default drive name*. The default drive is the one that OS/2 prints in its prompt. For example, if the prompt is [C:\], the default drive is the C drive.

You can change the default drive by typing in the drive name followed by a colon. For example:

```
C:
```

will make the C drive the default drive.

```
A:
```

will make the A drive the default drive.

Because related files are usually stored within the same directory, you will quite often work with files within one directory for some period. Instead of typing in the full path name every time you want to manipulate a file in that directory, you can tell OS/2 that all further file references, unless given a specific path, refer to that directory. The directory is called the *default directory* or *current working directory*. You tell OS/2 the name of the default directory with the **CHDIR** command. Its format is:

```
CHDIR directory_name
```

where *directory_name* is the name of the directory — which can include the complete path from the root directory — that you want to make the default directory. For example, suppose all of the files relating to a particular report you are preparing are in the \BUSINESS\PSGPROJ directory. You could type:

```
CHDIR \BUSINESS\PSGPROJ
```

If you then typed **DIR**, the files in the \BUSINESS\PSGPROJ directory would be listed. Note that because no drive name was specified, the directory is assumed to be in the default drive.

Note that when you change the default directory, the prompt also changes. The prompt lists the default drive and the default directory (Figure 3-9).

Directory Name Shortcuts

So far you have specified directories by given the path to the directory from the root directory. You have done this by starting the directory name with a \, meaning start at the root. If you leave out the \, the path starts from the default directory. For example, suppose the current directory is \BUSINESS and that it contains a directory called PSGPROJ. Typing CHDIR PSGPROJ would have the same result as typing CHDIR \BUSINESS\PSGPROJ.

You can also use .. to refer to the *parent directory*. The parent directory is the directory that contains another directory. For example, BUSINESS is the parent of PSGPROJ. The root directory is the parent of the BUSINESS directory. If you were in the \BUSINESS\PSGPROJ directory, CHDIR .. would switch you to the \BUSINESS directory.

```
[C:\] a:
[A:\] c:
[C:\] chdir language
[C:\LANGUAGE]
```

Figure 3-9 Illustration of changes drives and directories.

You can use these directory shortcuts with the other OS/2 commands as well. For example, DIR .. will list all of the files in the parent directory. DIR ..*.CMD will list all batch files in the parent directory (Figure 3-10).

Creating and Removing Directories

Directories are easy to create and remove. Use the **MKDIR** command to make a directory. Its format is:

    MKDIR *directory_name*

where *directory_name* is the name of the directory you want to create. You can specify a drive and a path name if you want.

```
[C:\DEMOS]

[C:\DEMOS] dir

Volume in drive C is DISK1_VOL1
Directory of C:\DEMOS

    .              <DIR>        10-14-87   11:28p
    ..             <DIR>        10-14-87   11:28p
README               182         5-27-87   12:00a
EXAMPLES         <DIR>        10-14-87   11:29p
APPS             <DIR>        10-14-87   11:30p
DIR        TS3         0        10-19-87   11:45a

      6 File(s)     9674752 bytes free

[C:\DEMOS]

[C:\DEMOS] dir ..\os2sys\*.cmd

Volume in drive C is DISK1_VOL1
Directory of C:\OS2SYS

INITENV   CMD       139      8-01-87   12:00a
INSTBOOT  CMD       608      8-01-87   12:00a
INSTFLP   CMD       775      8-01-87   12:00a
STARTUP   CMD       690      8-01-87   12:00a

      4 File(s)     9674752 bytes free

[C:\DEMOS]
```

Figure 3-10 Directory name shortcuts.

For example, to make a directory called TEST in the root directory of the C drive, you would enter:

    MKDIR C:\TEST

To put the test directory in the default drive and directory, you would enter:

    MKDIR TEST

You could place TEST in the parent directory by typing:

    MKDIR ..\TEST

You can create several directories at once by supplying **MKDIR** with a list of directory names. For example,

```
MKDIR ..\TEST REPLY
```

will put a directory named TEST in the parent directory and a directory named REPLY in the current directory.

To remove a directory, you use the **RMDIR** command. Its format is:

```
RMDIR directory_name
```

where *directory_name* is the name of the directory to remove. As a safeguard, you cannot remove a directory if it has files in it. You might want to use **DIR** to check a directory before you remove it.

If a directory has files in it and you are sure that you want to get rid of all of the files and the directory, type:

```
DEL directory_name
```

and answer *y* when OS/2 asks if you are sure. Then, type:

```
RMDIR directory_name
```

As with **MKDIR**, you can remove several directories at once by giving **RMDIR** a list of directories to remove (Figure 3-11).

Copying Files

You will work with files all of the time. One thing you will need to do often is copy files. You do this when you want to load a file from a floppy disk, when you want to back up a file or when you want to put a copy of a file on floppy so that you can use it with a different computer.

The **COPY** command copies files. Its format is:

```
[C:\]

[C:\] mkdir test

[C:\] dir test

Volume in drive C is DISK1_VOL1
Directory of C:\TEST
    .           <DIR>      10-19-87  11:46a
    ..          <DIR>      10-19-87  11:46a

    2 File(s)    9670656 bytes free

[C:\]

[C:\] rd test

[C:\] dir test

Volume in drive C is DISK1_VOL1
Directory of C:\

DOS0002: The system cannot find the file specified.

[C:\]
```

Figure 3-11 MKDIR and RMDIR.

```
COPY source_file   destination_file
```

where *source_file* is the name of the file that you want to copy. This can include a drive name, path name, and file name. You can use wild cards in the file name. *Destination_file* is the name of the file you want to copy the source file to. It can include a drive name, path name, and file name. If you give it a file name, the copy of the source file will have that name. If you don't give it a file name (that is, if only a drive or path is specified), the file will have the same name as the source file. Here are some examples:

```
COPY C:\BUSINESS\INFO.LET A:\BUSINFO.LET
```

will take the file INFO.LET from the BUSINESS directory on the C drive and place a copy of it, named BUSINFO.LET, in the root directory of the A drive.

```
COPY C:\BUSINESS\INFO.LET A:\
```

will take the file INFO.LET from the BUSINESS directory on the C drive and place a copy of it, named INFO.LET, in the root directory of the A drive.

```
COPY C:\BUSINESS\INFO.LET A:
```

will take the file INFO.LET from the BUSINESS directory on the C drive and place a copy of it, named INFO.LET, in the default directory of the A drive.

```
COPY C:*.* A:
```

will copy all files from the default directory in the C drive to the default directory of the A drive, preserving the file names.

```
COPY C:*.LET A:*.TXT
```

will copy all files in the default directory of the C drive that have the extension LET and place them in the default directory of the A drive, changing their extension to TXT (Figure 3-12).

Deleting Files

If you will no longer use a file, you might want to delete it. This will give you more room on your disk. Be sure, however, that you will never want to use the file again. If you are not certain, copy the file to a disk as a backup. If you need the file again, you can recopy it from the disk.

Use the **DEL** command to delete a file. Its format is:

```
[C:\]

[C:\] copy c:\os2\help.* a:

C:\OS2\HELP.BAT
C:\OS2\HELP.CMD
        2 file(s) copied.

[C:\]

[C:\] dir a:help.*

Volume in drive A is TESTDISK
Directory of A:\

HELP     BAT      444   6-26-87   9:44a
HELP     CMD      439   6-18-87   5:11p

    2 File(s)      122880 bytes free

[C:\]
```

Figure 3-12 COPY.

```
DEL file_name
```

where *file_name* is the name of the file to delete. You can give a drive name, path name, and wild cards. Here are some examples:

```
DEL BUSINFO.LET
```

will erase the file called BUSINFO.LET.

```
DEL BUSINFO.*
```

will erase all files whose name starts with BUSINFO.

```
[C:\]

[C:\] dir a:help


Volume in drive A is TESTDISK
Directory of A:\

HELP     BAT     444    6-26-87    9:44a
HELP     CMD     439    6-18-87    5:11p

    2 File(s)     122880 bytes free

[C:\] del a:help.*

[C:\] dir a:help.*

Volume in drive A is TESTDISK
Directory of A:\

DOS0002: The system cannot find the file specified.

[C:\]
```

Figure 3-13 Deleting files.

```
DEL *.*
```

will erase all files.

You can also supply a list of files to delete. For example, the following will delete all files with the .TXT extension, the file BILLG.LET, and all files starting with BEER:

```
DEL *.TXT BILLG.LET BEER*.*
```

Be very careful if you use wild cards with **DEL**. It is very easy to accidentally delete crucial information but very hard to get it back (Figure 3-13).

Summary

- There are four common types of floppy disks. These are low- and high-density 5 1/4-inch disks and low- and high-density 3 1/2-inch disks.
- Hard disks store more information than floppy disks and can access it more quickly.
- Disks are broken up into sides, tracks, sectors, bytes, and clusters. Only advanced users need to deal with these terms.
- Information is saved on disks in files.
- Disk drives, peripherals, and files are given names.
- Use floppy disks for backing up files, transferring files, saving files that you won't use much, and loading new files.
- Before you use a new floppy disk, you must format it.
- Directories organize disks into smaller, more usable units. Directories can contain files and other directories. Like files, directories have names.
- Plan your disk organization so that you will easily be able to find files. Break it into directories that hold related files.
- Use the **TREE** command to examine a disk's directory organization. Use the **DIR** command to see the files within a particular directory. Use the **TREE /F** command to list all files on the disk.
- The wild cards, * and ?, let you specify a broad range of files to examine.
- If you don't specify a drive or directory, the default drive or the default directory will be used. Change the default drive by typing the drive name followed by a colon. Change the default directory with the **CHDIR** command.
- Create and remove directories with the **MKDIR** and **RMDIR** commands. You can remove a directory only if it doesn't have any files in it.
- Copy files using the **COPY** command. Delete files using the **DEL** command. Be very careful if you use wild cards with **DEL**.

4

The Basics

In this chapter you'll learn how to use the OS/2 Session Manager and how to enter commands at the OS/2 prompt. You'll also learn how to run OS/2 and DOS programs.

Starting OS/2

To start OS/2, simply turn on your computer. The hard disk will whir, some messages will appear, and after a minute or so, OS/2 will start.[1]

The Session Manager

Once OS/2 starts, the *Session Manager* will appear on the screen.[2] The Session Manager is a unique feature of OS/2 that shows what programs are currently running and that lets

---

[1] If you need to restart OS/2 at any point, press the Control (Ctrl), Alt, and Delete (Del) keys at the same time.
[2] If OS/2 has been tailored to automatically start applications, an application screen might appear instead of the Session Manager. If this happens, just press Ctrl-Escape (Esc) to use the Session Manager.

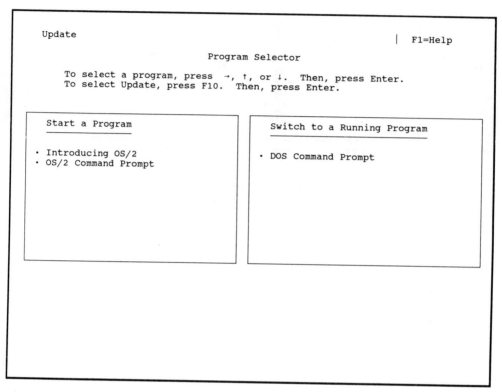

```
 Update                                          | F1=Help
                          Program Selector
     To select a program, press  →, ↑, or ↓.  Then, press Enter.
     To select Update, press F10.  Then, press Enter.


   ┌─────────────────────────────┐      ┌──────────────────────────────┐
   │ Start a Program             │      │ Switch to a Running Program  │
   │ ─────────────────           │      │ ──────────────────────────   │
   │                             │      │                              │
   │ • Introducing OS/2          │      │ • DOS Command Prompt         │
   │ • OS/2 Command Prompt       │      │                              │
   │                             │      │                              │
   │                             │      │                              │
   │                             │      │                              │
   │                             │      │                              │
   │                             │      │                              │
   │                             │      │                              │
   └─────────────────────────────┘      └──────────────────────────────┘
```

Figure 4-1 Session Manager's opening screen.

you switch to different programs. It also lets you start new programs, and it has a built-in HELP facility.

The Session Manager has two columns: **Start a Program** and **Switch to a Running Program** (Figure 4-1). Since OS/2 is a multitasking operating system, several programs can run at once. The **Switch to a Running Program** column lists all of the programs that are currently running. Each program is said to be running in its own *screen group.* When you select a program from the list, it appears on the screen. You can then enter commands from the keyboard and its output will appear on the screen. The other programs are still running, but because there is only one keyboard and screen, you can only type commands to them and see their output when you select them through the Session Manager.

To switch to a running program, just use the mouse or arrow keys to move the cursor to the name of the program. Then

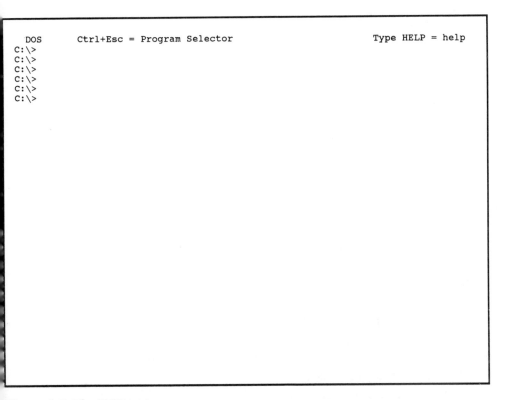

```
    DOS         Ctrl+Esc = Program Selector              Type HELP = help
  C:\>
  C:\>
  C:\>
  C:\>
  C:\>
  C:\>
```

Figure 4-2 The DOS screen.

press the left mouse button or the Enter key. The program you select will appear on the screen. For example, when you first turn on the computer, the only programs running are OS/2 and the DOS compatibility screen group.[3] To run a DOS program, move the cursor to the *DOS Command Prompt* entry and hit Enter. The DOS screen will appear (Figure 4-2). From the DOS prompt, you can run any DOS commands or programs. (Entering commands from the DOS and OS/2 prompts is discussed later in this chapter.)

Try this out. Move the cursor to DOS Command Prompt and hit the Enter key. When the DOS prompt appears, type DIR. A list of all the files in the current directory will appear.

---

[3] In Chapter 10 you'll learn how to make OS/2 automatically start up several programs when you turn on the computer.

Returning to the Session Manager

Whenever you want to return to the Session Manager, hit Ctrl-Esc. For example, suppose you are working with a program that is doing a lot of calculations. You want to start a new program so that you can continue working. To return to the session manager, you would just hit Ctrl-Esc.

Starting a New Program

To start a program, move the cursor to the name of a program in the **Start a Program** column. Then hit Return. For example, suppose you want to run the **Introducing OS/2** program. Move the cursor to the **Introducing OS/2** bar and hit Return. The program will start.

If you want to start a program that isn't listed in the **Start a Program** list, move to the **OS/2 Command** Prompt entry in the **Start a Program** list. Hit Enter, and when the OS/2 prompt appears, enter the name of the program to run, as discussed later in this chapter.

Switching between Programs

When you run several programs at once, you will probably need to switch between them. There are two ways to do this. The first way is to hit Ctrl-Esc to return to the Session Manager, then select the program to switch to. The second way is to hit Alt-Esc. This lets you toggle through screen groups. When you hit Alt-Esc from within a screen group, the next screen group in the **Running Program** list will appear on the screen. Keep hitting Alt-Esc until the program you want appears on the screen.

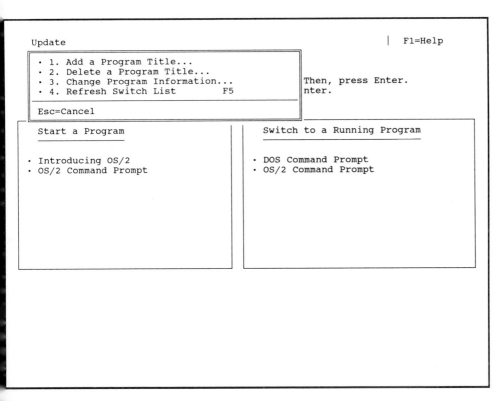

```
 Update                                           | F1=Help

  ┌──────────────────────────────────────────┐
  │ · 1. Add a Program Title...               │
  │ · 2. Delete a Program Title...            │
  │ · 3. Change Program Information...        │Then, press Enter.
  │ · 4. Refresh Switch List          F5      │nter.
  ├──────────────────────────────────────────┤
  │ Esc=Cancel                                │
┌─└──────────────────────────────────────────┘──────────────────────┐
│ Start a Program              │ Switch to a Running Program         │
│ ────────────────             │ ──────────────────────────          │
│                              │                                     │
│ · Introducing OS/2           │ · DOS Command Prompt                │
│ · OS/2 Command Prompt        │ · OS/2 Command Prompt               │
│                              │                                     │
│                              │                                     │
│                              │                                     │
│                              │                                     │
└──────────────────────────────┴─────────────────────────────────────┘
```

Figure 4-3 Update menu of the Session Manager.

Adding New Programs to the 'Start a Program' List

You should add your word processor and spreadsheet programs, as well as any other programs that you often run, to the menu of programs in the **Start a Program** list. To do so, use the **Update** option. Press the F10 key. This pulls down the **Update** menu (Figure 4-3).

Hit the Enter key to move to the menu, then hit the Enter key again to select the **Add a Program Title** option. A new menu will appear on the screen (Figure 4-4). Type in the title of the program. This is the name that will appear in the **Start a Program** list. When you are finished typing, *do not hit Enter.* Instead, hit the down arrow key to move to the *Program Path-*

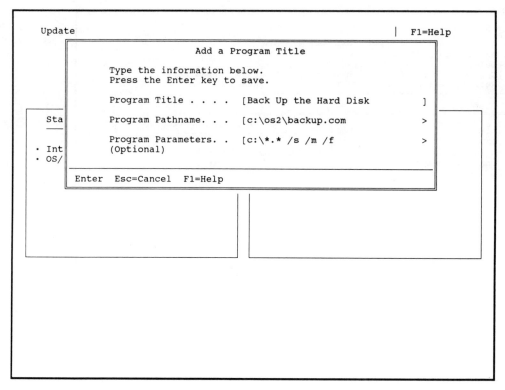

Figure 4-4 Adding an item to the Start a Program screen of the Session Manager.

name entry. Type in the complete name of the program file to run. You can find this from the documentation that comes with your software. If there are special parameters to pass to your program (these are called command line parameters and can include special flags or file names), hit the down arrow key and type them in the *Program Parameters* box, then hit Enter. If there are no command line parameters, simply hit Enter.

For example, suppose you want to add an item to the **Start a Program** list that will automatically back up your hard disk. You could type in the information shown in Figure 4.4. (The BACKUP command is discussed in detail in Chapter 6.)

When you return to the Session Manager, the new program title will appear in the **Start A Program** list (Figure 4-5).

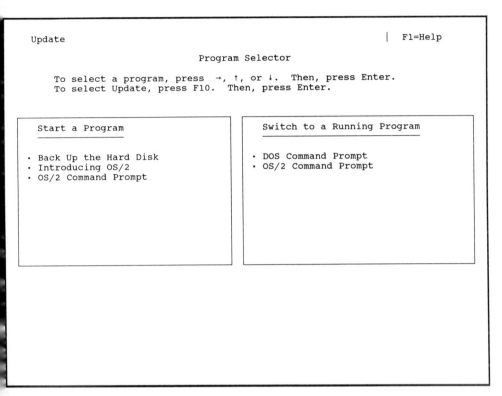

```
Update                                              |  F1=Help
                        Program Selector
     To select a program, press  →, ↑, or ↓.  Then, press Enter.
     To select Update, press F10.  Then, press Enter.


   ┌─────────────────────────────┐      ┌─────────────────────────────┐
   │ Start a Program             │      │ Switch to a Running Program │
   │ ─────────────               │      │                             │
   │                             │      │  · DOS Command Prompt       │
   │ · Back Up the Hard Disk     │      │  · OS/2 Command Prompt      │
   │ · Introducing OS/2          │      │                             │
   │ · OS/2 Command Prompt       │      │                             │
   │                             │      │                             │
   │                             │      │                             │
   │                             │      │                             │
   │                             │      │                             │
   │                             │      │                             │
   └─────────────────────────────┘      └─────────────────────────────┘
```

Figure 4-5 Session Manager's screen after an item is added.

Changing Information in the 'Start a Program' List

Sometimes you may need to change information in the **Start a Program** list. For example, you may want to change the parameters you pass to the program or, because of an update, the name of a program might change. You can do this with the **Change Program Information** option of the update menu (see Figure 4-3). Hit F10 to get the **Update** menu, then hit Enter and use the down arrow key to move to **Change Program Information**. Now hit Enter. A new menu will appear on the screen (Figure 4-6). Use the arrow keys to select the program that you want to change. Then hit Return. Another menu will appear on the screen (Figure 4-7) that lets you edit the information you typed with the **Add a Program Title** command. Use the up and down arrows to move between

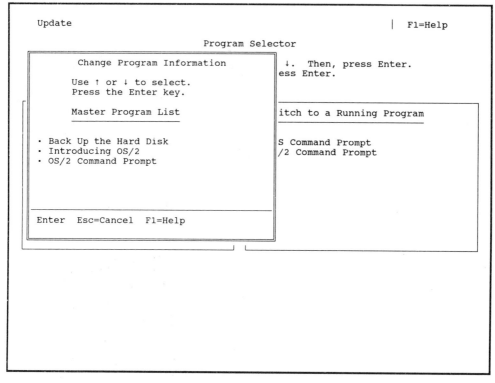

Figure 4-6 Change Program Information window with available options.

the title, pathname, and parameters entries. Use the left and right arrows to move within the entries. When you are finished making modifications, hit Enter.

Deleting Programs from the 'Start a Program' List

You can easily remove programs from the **Start a Program** list. Hit F10 and then Enter to get to the **Update** menu. Use the down arrow key to move to item 2, **Delete a Program Title**, and hit Enter. When the new menu appears on the screen (Figure 4-8), use the up and down arrow keys to select the name of the program to remove. Then hit the Enter key. A special menu will pop up to make sure you really want to delete the program from the **Start a Program** list (Figure 4-9). Hit

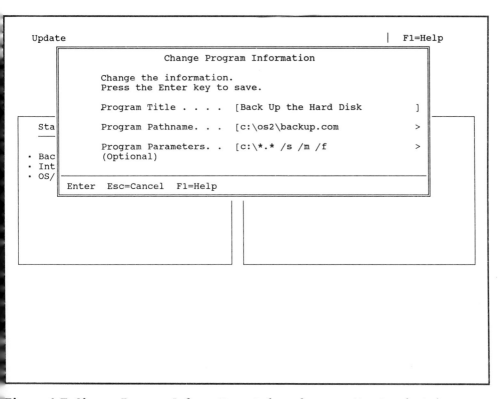

```
 Update                                          |  F1=Help
        ┌─────────────────────────────────────────────┐
        │         Change Program Information           │
        │                                              │
        │   Change the information.                    │
        │   Press the Enter key to save.               │
        │                                              │
        │   Program Title . . . .  [Back Up the Hard Disk    ]
   ┌────┤                                              ├────┐
   │ Sta│   Program Pathname. . .  [c:\os2\backup.com      > │    │
   │    │                                              │    │
   │    │   Program Parameters. .  [c:\*.* /s /m /f        > │    │
 • Bac│   (Optional)                                 │
 • Int│                                              │
 • OS/│ ─────────────────────────────────────────────│
        │ Enter   Esc=Cancel   F1=Help                 │
        └─────────────────────────────────────────────┘
```

Figure 4-7 Change Program Information window after an option is selected.

Enter if you really want to delete the program from the list, or hit Esc if you have changed your mind.

Note: If you delete a program from the **Start a Program** list, OS/2 doesn't erase the program from the disk. You can always put the program back into the **Start a Program** list by using the **Add a Program Title** option.

Getting Help about OS/2 in the Session Manager

If you need help with running OS/2, but your copy of *Running OS/2*, isn't nearby, you can run through the **Introducing OS/2** program.[4] Get into the Session Manager and move the

---

[4] At this point, this program is a special feature of IBM OS/2.

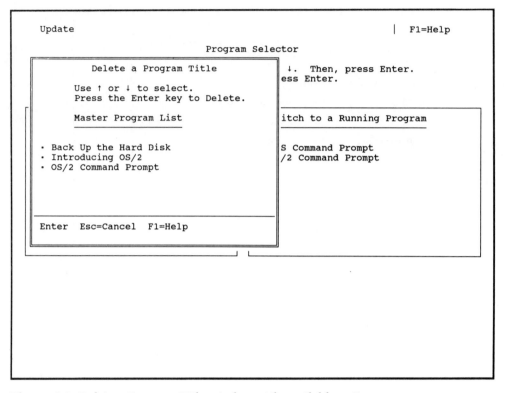

Figure 4-8 Delete a Program Title window with available options.

cursor to the **Introducing OS/2** option in the **Start a Program** column. Then hit Enter. Follow the **Introducing OS/2** instructions.

Getting Help about Using the Session Manager

While you are in the Session Manager, you can hit the F1 key at any time to get help with using the Session Manager. A window will pop up and give you information about your command options. For example, if you hit F1 while the cursor is in the **Start a Program** column, the pop-up window will contain information about starting programs. You can use the up and down arrows, the Page Up (PgUp) and Page Down (PgDn)

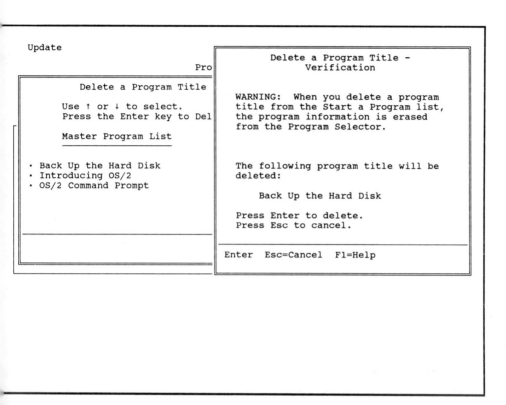

Figure 4-9 Delete a Program Title-Verification window.

keys, or a mouse to scroll through the help information. Hit Esc when you are finished.

After you hit F1, there are several other help screens you can load. Hit F9 to get a list of the Session Manager function keys (Figure 4-11). Hit F5 to get a list of all available help topics (Figure 4-12). To get more information about an item in the list, use the up and down arrow keys to move to that item, then hit the space bar. A new window containing information about that item will appear on the screen. For example, if you wanted general help information, you could move the cursor down to **General Help** and then hit the space bar. The **General Help Information** window will appear (Figure 4-13). Hit Esc when you are finished reading it. You can then choose another topic or hit Esc again to leave.

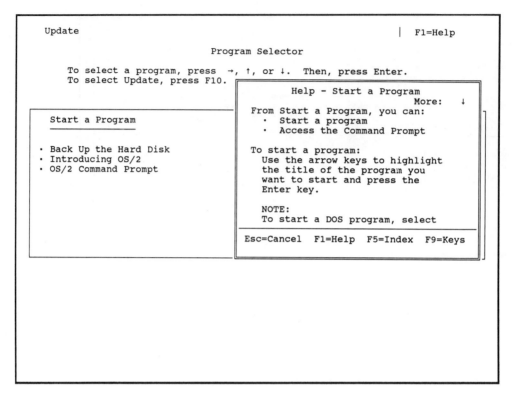

```
Update                                            |  F1=Help
                        Program Selector
     To select a program, press  →, ↑, or ↓.  Then, press Enter.
     To select Update, press F10.
                                ┌──────────────────────────────────┐
                                │       Help - Start a Program      │
                                │                       More:    ↓  │
                                │  From Start a Program, you can:   │
     ┌──────────────────────────┤   •  Start a program              │
     │  Start a Program         │   •  Access the Command Prompt    │
     │  ─────────────────       │                                   │
     │                          │  To start a program:              │
     │  • Back Up the Hard Disk │   Use the arrow keys to highlight │
     │  • Introducing OS/2      │   the title of the program you    │
     │  • OS/2 Command Prompt   │   want to start and press the     │
     │                          │   Enter key.                      │
     │                          │                                   │
     │                          │  NOTE:                            │
     │                          │  To start a DOS program, select   │
     │                          ├──────────────────────────────────┤
     │                          │ Esc=Cancel  F1=Help  F5=Index  F9=Keys │
     │                          └──────────────────────────────────┘
     └──────────────────────────┘
```

Figure 4-10 Help-Start a Program window.

The Typical Appearance of the Session Manager

While you are working with OS/2, typically there will be many programs in the **Start a Program** list and many programs in the **Running Program** list (Figure 4-14). As mentioned above, you can make any of the running programs appear on the screen by moving to the Session Manager (with Ctrl-Esc) and selecting the program name from the **Running Program** list, or by toggling through programs with the Alt-Esc key. To start a new program, go to the Session Manager with Ctrl-Esc, then select a program name from the **Start a Program** list. You can have several copies of the same program running at one time.

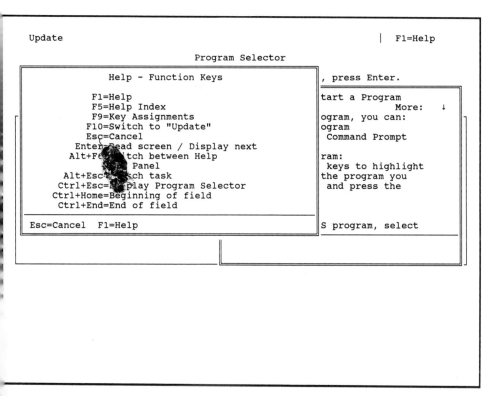

Figure 4-11 List of Session Manager function keys.

Differences between the IBM and MS OS/2 Session Manager

You may find slight differences between the MS and IBM OS/2 Session Managers. These are primarily in appearance; both function the same. Figure 4-15 shows the slight difference in the layout between the two Session Managers.

Entering Commands from the OS/2 Prompt

When you start an OS/2 or DOS screen group from the Session Manager, an OS/2 or DOS prompt will appear on the

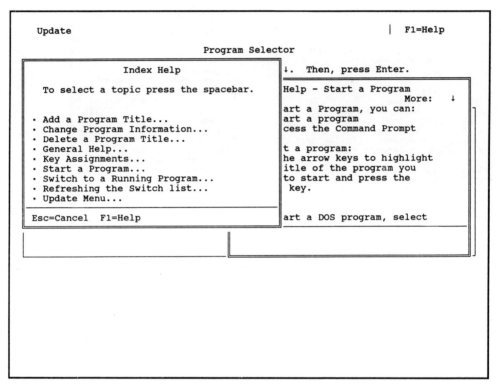

Figure 4-12 List of all available Help topics.

screen. The OS/2 prompt is always within square brackets and contains the current drive and path name. For example, when you first start an OS/2 screen, the prompt will be *[C:\]* (Figure 4-16). With IBM OS/2, the top line of the screen will also indicate that you are in OS/2, as seen in Figure 4.16. MS OS/2 will not necessarily have this feature.

When you are in the DOS compatibility mode screen group, a DOS prompt will appear on the screen. With IBM OS/2 this looks like the normal DOS prompt, and a line at the top of the screen indicates that you are in DOS compatibility mode (see Figure 4.2). With MS OS/2 the prompt might be *[Real C:\]* instead (Figure 4-17).

Whenever you see the prompt, you can enter an OS/2 (or DOS) command or run a program. You have already learned

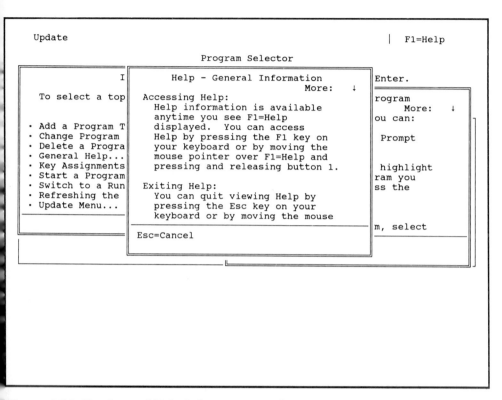

Figure 4-13 The General Help Information window.

many OS/2 commands in Chapter 3. The rest of the OS/2 and DOS compatibility mode commands are discussed in Chapter 6.

To enter a command, simply type it on the keyboard and then hit Return. For example, suppose you want a list of all files in the current drive and directory. Just type **DIR** and hit Return (Figure 4-18).

As with DOS, if you make a mistake while typing, you can easily correct the problem without retyping in the whole line. OS/2 remembers the last line that you typed and has built-in commands to edit this line. The editing commands let you copy characters from the previous line to the current line. The editing commands use the function keys shown in the table that follows:

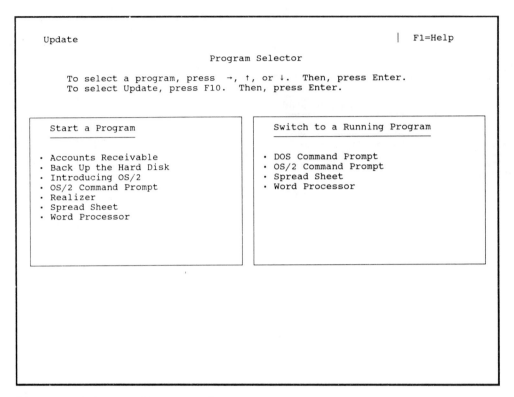

Figure 4-14 Session Manager with more options.

Key	Action
F1	Copies one character from previous command
F2*x*	Copies all characters up to the next occurrence of *x*
F3	Copies the remaining characters in the line
F4*x*	Skips the characters in the old command until the next occurrence of *x*
DEL	Skips over one character in the old command
INS	Toggles insert mode, which is initially off
Escape	Cancels the current command; does not affect the command buffer

For example, if the last OS/2 command you typed was:

```
DIR C:BAKERY C:\DINNCES
```

```
 Update                                       |  F1=Help
                         Program Selector
 Use ← or → to move between Start a Program and Switch to a Running Program.
 Use ↑ or ↓ to select, then press Enter. Press F10 then Enter to Update lists.


 ┌──────────────────────────────┐   ┌──────────────────────────────┐
 │  Start a Program             │   │  Switch to a Running Program │
 │  ──────────────              │   │  ──────────────────────────  │
 │                              │   │                              │
 │ •* OS/2 Command Prompt *     │   │ •MS-DOS Command Prompt       │
 │                              │   │ •CMD.EXE                     │
 │                              │   │ •* OS/2 Command Prompt *     │
 │                              │   │                              │
 │                              │   │                              │
 │                              │   │                              │
 │                              │   │                              │
 │                              │   │                              │
 └──────────────────────────────┘   └──────────────────────────────┘
```

Figure 4-15 MS OS/2 Session Manager screen.

but you meant to type:

```
DIR C:BAKERY C:\FINANCES
```

you could copy all characters up to the second D, type in an F, copy all characters up to the N, insert an A, and copy the rest of the line. You would type:

F2D
F
F2N
F2N
INS
A
F3

```
   OS/2      Ctrl+Esc = Program Selector              Type HELP = help
   [C:\]
   [C:\]
   [C:\]
   [C:\]
   [C:\]
```

Figure 4-16 IBM OS/2 screen prompt.

The line

```
DIR C:BAKERY C:\FINANCES
```

would now appear next to the prompt. You could then hit Enter to execute the command.

Running a Program

All programs have names. To run a program, you simply type in the name of the program at the OS/2 prompt. Documentation for programs will tell the name you type to run the program. For example, suppose the name of your word proces-

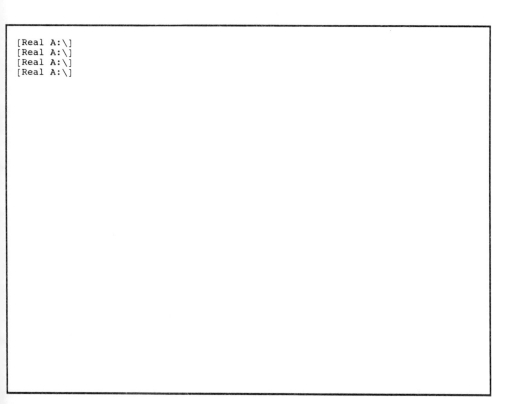

```
[Real A:\]
[Real A:\]
[Real A:\]
[Real A:\]
```

Figure 4-17 MS OS/2 screen prompt.

sor is WP, and you are in the directory in which WP is located. To run your word processor, you simply type WP and hit Enter.

Special Keys

There are several special OS/2 commands you might want to use. A table of these special keys follows:

Special Key	Function
Ctrl-Break	Stops a program
Ctrl-Print Screen (Prt Sc)	Causes all following output to be echoed to the printer

```
[C:\] dir

Volume in drive C is DISK1_VOL1
Directory of C:\

AUTOEXEC BAT      412   10-16-87    9:59a
CONFIG   SYS      350   10-14-87    8:09p
STARTUP  CMD      100   10-14-87    8:09p
OS2INIT  CMD      212   10-14-87    8:15p
DOS           <DIR>     10-14-87   11:13p
UTILITY       <DIR>     10-14-87   11:14p
OS2SYS        <DIR>     10-14-87   11:23p
OS2           <DIR>     10-14-87   11:24p
LANGUAGE      <DIR>     10-14-87   11:32p
TOOLS         <DIR>     10-14-87   11:26p
INCLUDE       <DIR>     10-14-87   11:27p
LIB           <DIR>     10-14-87   11:28p
INIT          <DIR>     10-14-87   11:28p
DEMOS         <DIR>     10-14-87   11:28p
SOURCES       <DIR>     10-14-87   11:30p
CONFIG        <DIR>     10-14-87   11:36p
WP            <DIR>     10-14-87   11:36p
WINDOWS       <DIR>     10-14-87   11:39p

     18 File(s)     9691136 bytes free

[C:\]
```

Figure 4-18 Entering a command at the OS/2 prompt.

Prt Sc	Causes the current screen to be printed on the printer
Pause	Pauses the display; hit any key to resume displaying
Ctrl-Esc	Switch to the Session Manager
Alt-Esc	Switch to the next screen group in the active program list

Error Messages

If an error occurs when you type a command, an error message will appear on the screen. These messages start with the word DOSxxxx, where xxxx is a number. The messages also display a short description of the problem. If you want more information about the error, you can type:

```
HELPMSG DOSxxxx or xxxx
```

where *xxxx* is the name of the error message.
   With IBM OS/2 you can also type:

```
HELP DOSxxxx or xxxx
```

where *xxxx* is the name of the error message. For example, suppose you don't have a drive named Q on your system. If you typed:

```
DIR Q:
```

OS/2 would display:

```
DOS0015: The system cannot find the drive specified.
```

If you wanted more information, you could type:

```
HELPMSG 15
```

and OS/2 would display:

```
DOS0015: The system cannot find the drive specified.

EXPLANATION: The drive specified does not exist on
your system or is incorrect. ACTION: Retry the com-
mand using a correct drive letter.
```

Ending an OS/2 Screen Group

When you start a program using the Session Manager, the program's screen group will disappear after the program finishes. For example, if you start your word processor from the Session Manager, when you exit the word processor, its screen group will disappear and you will return to the Session Manager.

If you start a program from the OS/2 prompt, however, the screen group won't disappear after the program finishes. Instead, the OS/2 prompt will appear again. If you want to end an OS/2 screen group, type **EXIT** at the OS/2 prompt. The screen group will end and you will return to the session manager.

Summary

- Start OS/2 by turning on the computer.
- The Session Manager lets you start and switch to OS/2 programs and the DOS compatibility mode.
- Hit Ctrl-Esc to go to the Session Manager. Hit Alt-Esc to switch between running programs.
- While in the session manager, you can hit F1 to get help with the Session Manager.
- The OS/2 prompt indicates that OS/2 is active and waiting for an OS/2 command. The DOS prompt indicates that OS/2 is in the DOS compatibility mode.
- You can type in OS/2 commands or run programs from the prompt.
- Editing keys let you correct a line without retyping it.
- Use HELPMSG to get more information if you get an OS/2 error message.
- Type **EXIT** to close an OS/2 screen group.

5

Installing
Applications

Applications run faster and more efficiently if they are on the hard disk. In this chapter you'll see how to transfer applications to the hard disk.

Copying the Application Files

To install an application, you need to copy all of the application's files from the floppies it comes on to the hard disk, using the **COPY** command. The application's manual will tell you how to set up directories and what files to copy. The application may also come with an installation program that automatically installs all of the files.

If it is an application that you will use frequently, install it in the Session Manager's list of programs, as discussed in Chapter 4.

Using INSTAID

At some point Microsoft may release a program called INSTAID to help install and track installations. Run it by entering:

```
INSTAID x:application_name
```

where *x* is the drive in which the application disk is placed. INSTAID will read a special installation file and automatically load the necessary files. The installation menu will appear on your screen. Select the *Install a program* option. INSTAID will install the application, prompting you to insert disks when necessary.

   You can use INSTAID to see what applications you have installed and when they were loaded and updated. INSTAID will also help you remove applications.

Summary

- You can install applications by **COPY**ing all the application's files to your hard disk. The application's manual will instruct you on how to do this. The application might also include an installation program.
- If you use an application frequently, add its name to the session manager's **Start a Program** list.
- INSTAID will automatically install applications for you. It also tracks when applications were loaded and updated and helps you remove applications.

C H A P T E R
6

OS/2 Commands

This chapter contains an alphabetical list of all the OS/2 commands. Asterisks in each entry indicate whether the command will work in protected mode (the normal OS/2 mode) and/or the DOS compatibility mode. A description of the command, its format, comments, and examples follow. The following notation is used for command format:

CAPITALIZED WORDS	Actual OS/2 commands that you need to type
Italicized_parameters	Values that you need to substitute
[ ]	Indicate optional parameters
( ), ( )	Indicates a list of options from which only one can be chosen
[...]	Indicates that optionally an item can be repeated

For example,

```
ANSI [ (ON) (OFF) ]
```

means the following commands are valid: **ANSI, ANSI ON, ANSI OFF.**

ANSI   install ANSI support
  * Protected mode
    DOS compatibility mode

Function: This command allows programs to use the ANSI escape sequences for character control.

Format: ANSI [(ON) (OFF)]

Comments: The ANSI escape sequences are a series of special commands for setting display colors and controlling the display cursor. They are a device-independent way for programs to make attractive text screens.

If you type **ANSI ON**, then OS/2 will process ANSI escape sequences. If you type **ANSI OFF**, OS/2 will not process ANSI escape sequences. If you type **ANSI**, OS/2 will tell you if ANSI sequence processing is currently on or off. Documentation for applications should indicate whether they need ANSI support to be set to ON.

To process ANSI sequences in the DOS compatibility mode, you must include the ANSI.SYS driver in your CONFIG.SYS file. See Chapter 10 for more details.

Examples: To see if OS/2 currently processes ANSI sequences, type:
```
ANSI
```
To turn ANSI processing on, type:
```
ANSI ON
```
To turn ANSI processing off, type:
```
ANSI OFF
```

APPEND   Set search path for data files
    Protected mode
  * DOS compatibility mode

Function:	This function sets a path where DOS programs will look for data files.
Format:	APPEND [[*drive:*] *path*] [;[*drive*]*path*] [...] [/E]
Comments:	When programs look for data files, they look in the default drive and path or in the particular path specified. The **APPEND** command gives a list of directories that OS/2 will search if the file is not found in the default directory.

This command is very useful in that some programs were not designed to be run from a hard disk. When you transfer them to their own directory on a hard disk, they are not able to find data or overlay files. By specifying the application's path in the **APPEND** command, the program will find its files.

To stop OS/2 from searching for files in the **APPEND** directories, type:

```
APPEND ;
```

The **/E** option keeps the **APPEND** values in the environment until the **APPEND** command is cancelled. This lets batch files examine the **APPEND** directories by looking at %APPEND%.

If you use the **ASSIGN** command, use **APPEND** before **ASSIGN**.

See also:	DPATH
Examples:	Suppose your word processor keeps its overlay files in the directory C:\WS, but it expects them in the default directory. In addition, you keep spreadsheets in the directories C:\FINANCES, C:\BUSINESS\ESTS, and D:\PAYROLL, but you don't always remember which directory contains a particular spreadsheet. You could use:

```
APPEND C:\WS;C:\FINANCES;
  C:\BUSINESS\ESTS;D:\PAYROLL
```

ASSIGN   Assign a new drive letter to a disk drive
      Protected mode
   * DOS compatibility mode

Function: This function lets you use a different drive let-
                  ter name for a disk drive. For example, it will
                  automatically convert all references to the B
                  drive to references to the C drive.

Format: ASSIGN [actual_drive_name =
                  new_drive_name] [...]

Comments: This command lets programs which specifi-
                  cally use a particular drive use other drives.
                  For example, if a word processor always looks
                  for a temporary file on drive A, you can use
                  the ASSIGN command so that it will look on
                  drive C instead of drive A. To cancel the drive
                  assignment, type:
                  ASSIGN

                  This command is supported for com-
                  patibility purposes, but it will not necessarily
                  be supported in later OS/2 releases. Use the
                  SUBST command instead.

                  If you have used **ASSIGN**, make sure that
                  you cancel drive assignments before using
                  BACKUP, RESTORE, LABEL, JOIN, SUBST,
                  or **PRINT**.

See also: **SUBST**

Examples: Suppose that your word processor assumes
                  that its thesaurus is in the B drive. Instead,
                  you have placed it in the D drive. You could
                  type:
                  ASSIGN D = B
                  When you are finished, type:
                  ASSIGN

ATTRIB   Change file attribute
   * Protected mode
   * DOS compatibility mode

Function: This command changes the read-only or archive attribute of a file.

Format: ATTRIB [(+) (-) R] [(+) (-) A] [*drive_name:*]
[*path_name*] *file_name* [/S]

Comments: The read-only file attribute determines whether a file can be written to. If you set the read-only attribute, programs and users can read the file, but they cannot modify or delete it. Make a file read only by using the **+R** option. Make the file writable by using the **-R** option.

The archive attribute is used by backup programs to indicate if a file has been modified after it was last backed up. If the archive bit is set, backup routines (**BACKUP, RESTORE, XCOPY**) will back up the file. You can set this bit, using **+A**, to force a backup or clear it, using **-A**, to prevent a backup.

To check a file's attributes, type the **ATTRIB** command without the **R** or **A** options.

You can use wild cards with the file name. If you use the **/S** option, the ATTRIB command will be carried out on all files in subdirectories of the current directory.

Examples: To check the attributes of a file called MIRNA.LET in the current directory of the current drive, type:

```
ATTRIB MIRNA.LET
```

To make the file MIRNA.LET in the \LETTER directory of the current drive a read-only file, type:

```
ATTRIB +R \LETTER\MIRNA.LET
```

To clear the archive and read-only bits for all of the files in the \LETTER directory on the A drive and all of the files in subdirectories of A:\LETTER, type:

```
ATTRIB -A -R A:\LETTER\*.* /S
```

BACKUP   Back up files or a disk
   *   Protected mode
   *   DOS compatibility mode

Function: Backs up files from one disk to another. Typi-
                   cally used to back up a hard disk to floppies.

Format: BACKUP [*source_drive:*][*source_path*]
                      [*source_filename*] [*destination_drive:*] [/S]
                      [/M] [/A] [/F] [/D:*date*] [/T:*time*]
                      [/L:*log_file_name*]

Comments: The data on your hard disk is priceless. To
                   avoid disaster should your hard disk fail, you
                   should back up your hard disk regularly. For
                   example, you might want to back up your disk
                   every Friday afternoon. If you have not pur-
                   chased a program to make backups, use the
                   BACKUP command. While this command is
                   typically used to back up the hard disk, you
                   can use it to back up other disks as well.

                   As the backup is made, OS/2 will prompt
                   you to enter new floppies and warn you that
                   previous data on them will be destroyed. Set
                   aside a group of floppies that you will use only
                   for backups. You might need 20 or more flop-
                   pies in order to back up a hard disk. Label
                   each floppy sequentially as you use it. For ex-
                   ample, call the first disk Backup 1, the second
                   Backup 2, and so forth.

                   You can instruct **BACKUP** to back up a
                   single file, a directory, a group of files, or the
                   whole disk.

                   If you have used the **JOIN, ASSIGN**, or
                   SUBST commands, you should cancel them
                   before doing a backup.

                   The following table explains the BACKUP
                   options:

Option	Result
/S	Backs up subdirectories of the directory specified.
/M	Only backs up files that have changed since the last backup.
/A	Doesn't erase files that are already on the disks to which the backup is being made.
/F	Formats the floppies on which the backup is being made if they are not already formatted.
/D:*date*	Only backs up files that were modified on or after *date*.
/T:*time*	Only backs up files that were modified on or after *time*.
/L:*log_filename*	Stores information about the backup in *log_filename*. If this option is not used, a file called BACKUP.LOG is created in the root directory of the disk being backed up.

See also: **RESTORE**

Examples: If you want to back up all the files in the directory C:\LETTERS to floppies placed in the A drive, you could use:

`BACKUP C:\LETTERS A: /S /F`

To back up all of the files on your hard disk to floppies in the A drive, you could:

`BACKUP C:\ A: /S /F`

To back up files in the C:\LETTERS directory that you created after the afternoon of 4/25/88, you could use:

`BACKUP C:\LETTERS A: /F /D:4/25/88`
`/T:12:00`

BREAK   Set Ctrl-C and Ctrl-Break checking
     Protected mode
 *   DOS compatibility mode

Function: This command enables or disables Ctrl-C and
                   Ctrl-Break checking after OS/2 commands.

Format: BREAK [(ON) (OFF)]

Comments: You can use Ctrl-C or Ctrl-Break to stop a
                   program. Normally, programs only check to
                   see if these keys have been pressed when they
                   read or write to the screen or keyboard. If you
                   set **BREAK** to ON, OS/2 will check to see if
                   the Ctrl-Break or Ctrl-C keys have been
                   pressed before every internal function. This
                   slows a program down, but makes it much
                   easier to break out of programs. Set **BREAK**
                   to ON when you are debugging programs or if
                   you run programs that do a lot of calculations
                   but rarely read from or print to the screen. If
                   you mostly use applications such as spread-
                   sheets and word processors, set **BREAK** to
                   OFF. Note that this command is for DOS com-
                   patibility mode only.

                   The ON option causes OS/2 to check for
                   Ctrl-C and Ctrl-Break before every internal
                   OS/2 call. The OFF option instructs OS/2 not
                   to check for Ctrl-C and Ctrl-Break before
                   every internal OS/2 call. Using **BREAK** with
                   no parameters causes OS/2 to print the cur-
                   rent **BREAK** status.

Examples: Suppose you are about to run a program that
                   you just tested or that you are about to run a
                   scientific package with a lot of calculations
                   but little input and output. Set **BREAK** to **ON**
                   so that you will have a greater opportunity of
                   breaking out of the program if you need to:
                   BREAK ON

Suppose you have finished and now want to run your word processor. Cancel break checking with:

```
BREAK OFF
```

CHCP   Change code page
  * Protected mode
  * DOS compatibility mode

Function: This function selects or displays the code page.

Format: CHCP [*code_page_number*]

Comments: The code page determines what character set is used on the screen. Code pages define a systematic way to display foreign languages. Normally you will not need to change the code page.

You can select one of two code pages to use. The two code pages that you can select are defined in the CONFIG.SYS file. To see what code pages are available, type:

```
CHCP
```

To select a code page, type:

```
CHCP code_page_number
```

The following is a list of the valid numbers:

Code Page Number	Alphabet
437	United States
850	Multilingual
860	Portuguese
863	French-Canadian
865	Nordic

See also: **CODEPAGE** in CONFIG.SYS section of Chapter 10.

Examples: If you want to see what code pages are available, type:

CHCP

Suppose this responds that the current code page is 437 and that you can choose 437 or 860. If you wanted to choose the Portuguese code page, you would enter:

CHCP 860

CHDIR or **CD**   Change default directory
  * Protected mode
  * DOS compatibility mode

Function: This command changes or displays the default (current working) directory.

Format: CHDIR [[*drive_name:*]*path_name*]
               CD [[*drive_name:*]*path_name*]

Comments: This command changes the default directory. If you will be working with files mostly from the same directory, you should switch to that directory with **CHDIR**. All file references will be from that directory. For example, if the current working directory is PAYROLL, entering DIR *.* will display all of the files in the PAYROLL directory.

To see what the current directory is, type **CHDIR** without parameters. The prompt also displays the current directory.

To specify the new directory, you need to give a path. If you start the path with \, the path will be with respect to the root directory. If you don't start the path with \, the path will be with respect to the current directory.

See also: Chapter 3

Examples: Suppose you will be doing a lot of work in the C:\PAYROLL directory. To make this the current directory, you would enter:

CHDIR \PAYROLL

or as a shortcut,

```
CD \PAYROLL
```

Note how the prompt changes. (If you weren't currently in the C drive, first switch to the C drive by entering C:.) Now suppose that you will be doing a lot of work in the PSG directory in PAYROLL. You can switch to it by typing:

```
CD PSG
```

or

```
CD \PAYROLL\PSG
```

To go back to the PAYROLL directory, you could type:

```
CD ..
```

or

```
CD \PAYROLL
```

To go to the root directory, you would type:

```
CD \
```

If you want to see what the current directory is, type:

```
CD
```

To see what the current directory on the A drive is, type:

```
CD A:
```

CHKDSK   Check disk
  * Protected mode
  * DOS compatibility mode

Function: This function checks disk usage and reports any disk errors. In DOS compatibility mode, it reports the amount of memory available.

Format: CHKDSK [*drive_name*:]
   [[*path_name*]*file_name*] [/F] [/V]

Comments: This command scans the whole disk to determine how much of the disk is in use and if there are any file allocation errors. Occasionally, errant programs will not write files properly, and there will be parts of the disk marked in use that aren't being used by any files. **CHKDSK** will free up these areas if you request it to.

Use **CHKDSK** when you want to see how disk space is being used. Run it occasionally to fix up any disk problems that may have occurred.

In DOS compatibility mode, **CHKDSK** will report the total amount of memory and the amount of memory available for use.

If you specify a file name, which can include wild cards, **CHKDSK** will report how fragmented the file is. A fragmented file has parts of it stored in one area of the disk and other parts in another area. This makes it take longer to read or modify the file. There are several utilities for defragmenting files.

The **/F** option instructs OS/2 to fix any file errors that it finds. Don't use the **/F** option with the drive containing **CHKDSK**. So, if you want to do a CHKDSK C: /F, you should copy **CHKDSK** to a disk in drive A. Change to the A drive, then type:

CHKDSK C: /F

The **/V** option instructs OS/2 to print out the name of each file as it checks the disk.

Cancel any **JOIN** or **SUBST** drive assignments before using **CHKDSK**. Do not use the **/F** option while you are using background printing or spooling.

Examples: Suppose you want to see how much disk space is being used, and for what types of files. You could type:

CHKDSK

To do the same, but for a disk in the A drive, type:

CHKDSK A:

If **CHKDSK** reported problems with files on the C drive, you could fix them with:

```
CHKDSK C: /F
```

To see how fragmented the file C:\LAN-GUAGE\C\CC.EXE is, you could:

```
CHKDSK C:\LANGUAGE\C\CC.EXE
```

If you were in DOS compatibility mode and want to see how much memory is available, use:

```
CHKDSK
```

CLS   Clear the screen
* Protected mode
* DOS compatibility mode

Function:	This command clears the display screen.
Format:	CLS
Comments:	After you leave applications, your display screen may be cluttered. CLS clears the screen and returns the cursor to the upper left corner.
Examples:	Suppose you just used Ctrl-C to exit a program that drew text figures all over the screen. This makes it difficult for you to see the prompt. You could clear the display by typing:

```
CLS
```

CMD   Start a secondary command processor
* Protected mode
  DOS compatibility mode

Function:	This function starts a secondary command processor in the OS/2 Protected mode.
Format:	CMD [*drive_name:*][*path_name*] [(/C *string*) (/K *string*)]
Comments:	This function starts a secondary command processor. There is not much reason to execute this command from the OS/2 prompt; the typical use is from within a program.

The **/C** option instructs OS/2 to perform the commands listed in *string*, then return. This option allows a program to run OS/2 commands or other programs while it is running.

The **/K** option instructs OS/2 to perform the commands listed in *string*, then stay in the new command processor. This will display the OS/2 prompt on the screen. The user can then type OS/2 commands or run programs. To return to the previous command processor or the program, type **EXIT**.

You can specify a drive and path where OS/2 can find the secondary command processor.

One advantage of loading a new command processor is that you can change its environment without affecting the earlier environment.

See also: **COMMAND, EXIT, START**

Examples: You are writing a program in which you want the user to be able to use OS/2 internal commands (such as **DIR**). You do not want the user to have to leave the program to do so; you do not want the user to start a new session, because the path and enviroment would be different. You would **spawn** the following:

CMD /C dos_commands

This is similar to the C **system** command.

COMMAND   Start a secondary command processor
        Protected mode
    *   DOS compatibility mode

Function: This function starts a secondary command processor in the DOS compatibility mode.

Format: COMMAND [*drive_name:*][*path_name*] [(/P)
        (/C *string*)] [/E:*environment_size*]

Comments: This command is not normally executed at the DOS Compatibility Mode prompt. Instead, it is used by programs to create a *shell* option. This allows users to leave a program, execute

DOS commands, then return to the program exactly where they stopped working.

The **/P** option keeps the second command processor in memory until DOS is restarted. This option is used within the CONFIG.SYS file to allow a large environment space.

The **/C** option executes *string*, then returns immediately.

The **/E** option defines the environment size. The environment size must be 160 to 32,768 bytes. This is typically used with the **/P** option in the CONFIG.SYS file.

If you don't use the **/C** or **/P** option, the new processor will start, and the user can enter DOS compatibility mode commands and run programs. Typing **EXIT** returns to the original command shell or program.

See also: **CMD, SHELL** command in "CONFIG.SYS" section of Chapter 10.

Examples: Suppose you have written a word processor. You want to allow the user to execute OS/2 commands, such as **DIR, ERASE**, and **MKDIR**, or to run other programs without having to exit your program. You could **spawn** the following:

COMMAND

The user types **EXIT** to return to the program.

COMP   Compare contents of files
  * Protected mode
  * DOS compatibility mode

Function: This command compares the contents of one group of files with the contents of another group of files.

Format: COMP [*group1_drive_name*] [*group1_path_name*] [*group1_file_name*] [*group2_drive_name*][*group2_path_name*] [*group2_file_name*]

Comments: This command is used to compare the contents of one group of files with another. You can use this to see where you made changes in files. For example, you can compare an early version of source code with a later version. **COMP** indicates the locations in the files where different byte values are found.

You can use wild cards in the file names. **COMP** will compare the first match in the first group with the first match in the second group.

If you don't specify file names, **COMP** will compare all the files in the directory with all the files in the other directory.

COMP will stop after 10 differences have been found. You can compare files of different sizes.

Examples: Suppose you want to compare all of the Pascal files in the \H2OPROJ directory with their earlier versions, saved on a floppy. You could use:

```
COMP \H2OPROJ\*.PAS A:
```

COPY   Copy a group of files
  * Protected mode
  * DOS compatibility mode

Function: This command copies a file or group of files. The files can be copied to other disks or directories and can be renamed in the process. Files can also be concatenated.

Format: COPY [*source_drive_name:*] [*source_path_name*][*source_file_name*] [(/A) (/B)]
[*dest_drive_name:*] [*dest_path_name*] [*dest_file_name*] [(/A) (/B)] [/V]
COPY [*source1_drive_name:*] [*source1_path_name*] [*source1_file_name*]
[(/A) (/B)] +[*source2_drive_name:*] [*source2_path_name*] [*source2_file_name*]

[(/A) (/B)] [+ ...] [*dest_drive_name:*]
[*dest_path_name*] [*dest_file_name*]
[(/A) (/B)] [/V]

Comments: This command is very useful. It lets you make copies of files. You can copy files to other disks, for example, to make backups or to load new programs, or you can copy files to other directories. You can use the command to concatenate files together.

You can use wild cards in both the source and destination names. If you leave out the destination file name, the copied files will have the same names as the source files.

If a file with the same name already exists on the destination drive, **COPY** will overwrite it. You may want to use **XCOPY** instead.

In general, you do not need to use the **/A,** **/B**, or **/V** options. **/A** and **/B** are most useful for concatenating files.

The **/V** option instructs OS/2 to verify that the destination files were written correctly.

When used with a source file, the **/A** option instructs OS/2 that the file is an ASCII file. The file will be read until an end-of-file marker.

When used with a destination file, the **/A** option instructs OS/2 to add an end-of-file marker.

When used with a source file, the **/B** option instructs OS/2 that the file is a binary file. The file will be read until the bytes specified in its file size are copied.

When used with a destination file, the **/B** option prevents OS/2 from adding an end-of-file marker.

The **/A** and **/B** options apply until another **/A** or **/B** option is encountered.

See also: **XCOPY**, Copying Files section of Chapter 3

Examples: **Copying a single file, preserving the name—** To copy a single file, called MIRNA.LET, from C:\LETTERS to a floppy in the A drive, type:
```
COPY C:\LETTERS\MIRNA.LET A:
```

Copying a group of files, preserving the name—
To copy all .LET files from the A drive to the C:\LETTERS directory, use:
```
COPY A:*.LET C:\LETTERS
```

Copying one directory to another directory—
To copy all the files in the \LETTERS directory to the \OLDLET directory, do:
```
COPY \LETTERS \OLDLET
```

Copying a single file, changing its name—
To make a backup copy of LASERZAP.ASM, called LASERZAP.BAK, do the following:
```
COPY LASERZAP.ASM LASERZAP.BAK
```

Copying a group of files, changing their name—
To copy all files on the current directory in the A drive whose names start with FOUR to the current drive and directory, changing the first part of the name to FIVE, do:
```
COPY A:FOUR*.* FIVE*.*
```

Combining text files—
Suppose you have two address lists that you want to combine for a mailing list. You could do the following:
```
COPY NAMELIST.1 /A + NAMELIST.2
  NAMELIST.TOT
```

Combining binary files—
Suppose you have a program that reads a series of water pressure levels and stores them in a disk file in numeric (binary) format. To combine several weeks of readings into a new file, you could:

```
COPY READING.1 /B + READING.2 +
 READING.3 READING.TOT /B
```

Combining sets of files—
Suppose that you have a series of articles, indicated by extension .ART, and their bibliographies, indicated by extension .BIB. You want to add the .BIB file to each .ART file. You could:

```
COPY *.ART + *.BIB *.TOT
```

To combine all of the article files into one large file, you could:

```
COPY *.ART COMBINED.ART
```

DATE   Set or check the date
 * Protected mode
 * DOS compatibility mode

Function: This command sets or checks the date.
Format: DATE [*mm-dd-yy*]
Comments: This command sets or checks the date. If you type the command without parameters, OS/2 will display the date and ask you if you want to change it. Simply hit Return if you do not want to change it. If you change the date, the hardware clock date will be changed as well.

The way the date is printed depends upon the **COUNTRY** setting in the CONFIG.SYS file. European countries might use dd-mm-yy format instead of mm-dd-yy.

You can separate the month, day, and year entries by -, /, or .; *mm* can range between 1 and 12, *dd* between 1 and 31, and *yy* from 80 and 79 or 1980 and 2079. If you specify a day that doesn't exist, such as February 31, OS/2 will modify it.

See also: **COUNTRY** command in "CONFIG.SYS" section of Chapter 10.

Examples: Suppose you want to know what day it is. Type:

DATE

Suppose your computer thinks it is February 3, 1988, but it is really February 1, 1988. You could fix it by typing:

DATE 2-1-88

or correcting the date after entering **DATE**.

DEL   Erase a group of files
  * Protected mode
  * DOS compatibility mode

Function: Erase a file or group of files.

Format: DEL [[*drive_name*:] [*path_name*] [*file_name*]]
                [...]

Comments: DEL erases a file or group of files. You can use wild cards in the file name. Be very careful when you delete files. Since it is not easy to get back an erased file, be sure that you want to delete it before you do. Also be very careful when using wild cards in the file name.

                Deleting frees up disk space. You may want to look through your disk occasionally and delete files that you no longer need. If there is a chance that you will need the file, copy it to a floppy, then delete it from the hard disk.

                If you omit the file name, all files in the directory specified will be deleted. (However, you have to have either a file name or directory name or both.)

In DOS compatibility mode, you can only specify one file name (though it can contain wild cards).

Examples: **Deleting a single file—**

Suppose you saved an invoice, called PETERN.INV, that is no longer valid. You can erase it by typing:

```
DEL PETERN.INV
```

Deleting all files in a directory—

Suppose you have just saved all files in the \CLASSES\CS541 directory on a floppy disk. Since you will no longer be using these files, you can delete them by:

```
DEL \CLASSES\CS541
```

Deleting a group of files

Suppose you want to delete all files with the BAK extension and all files that start with TEMP. You could:

```
DEL *.BAK TEMP*.*
```

Deleting files in DOS compatibility mode

Suppose you want to delete all files with the BAK extension and all files that start with TEMP. You could:

```
DEL *.BAK
DEL TEMP*.*
```

DETACH Run a process in the background

  * Protected mode

   DOS compatibility mode

Function: This function causes a program to run in the background.

Format: DETACH *program_name* [*arguments*]

Comments   This command lets you run a program in the background. The program must be one that does not necessitate any keyboard input.

Program_name is the name of the program to run, and can include a drive and path name. *Arguments* is a list of any command line arguments to pass it.

The **DETACH** command is useful when you don't want to start another screen group to run a program. **DETACH**ing a program instead of starting a screen group also saves memory. A detached program must terminate by itself — the user is unable to terminate it.

Examples: Suppose you have a program that ray traces an image. It takes the input file and output file as command line arguments and uses no other input or output. This would be a good application to run as a detached process. You could:

```
DETACH \GRAPHICS\RAYTRACE D:PICTURE.DSC
    D:PICTURE.RYT
```

DIR   List files in a directory
 * Protected mode
 * DOS compatibility mode

Function: This command lists all the files and directories within a directory.

Format: DIR [[*drive_name:*] [*path_name*] [*file_name*]]
                [...] [/P] [/W]

Comments: This command lets you see what files are in a directory. If you don't specify a drive or path, the current drive and path are used. If you don't specify a file name, all files are listed. The file name can contain wild cards. Matching directory names are listed as well. They are indicated by a <DIR>.

The listing indicates the disk's name (volume), the size of the file, and the time and date it was last modified.

The **/P** option stops the listing every screenful. To continue listing, press any key.

The **/W** option lists the names only, in up to five columns across the screen.

In DOS compatibility mode, you can only specify one file or directory name at a time.

Examples: **Listing all files in the default directory—** Suppose the current directory is \LETTERS. You want to see all the files in it. You could type:

```
DIR /P
```

Listing all files in several directories— Suppose you want to see all files in the current directory, the parent directory, and the \BUSINESS directory. You could:

```
DIR *.* ..\*.* \BUSINESS\*.* /P
```

Note that in DOS compatibility mode, you would have to type:

```
DIR *.* /P
DIR ..\*.* /P
DIR \BUSINESS\*.* /P
```

List certain files only Suppose you only want to list files whose name begins with CHAP and whose extension is TXT or DOC. You could:

```
DIR CHAP*.TXT CHAP*.DOC /P
```

DISKCOMP   Compare two floppy disks
* Protected mode
* DOS compatibility mode

Function: This command compares, byte for byte, two floppy disks.

Format: DISKCOMP [*first_drive*] [*second_drive*]

Comments: This command is useful for verifying that one disk is an exact copy of another disk. You may want to do this after copying or mass copying a batch of disks using **DISKCOPY** or another direct image copier. Do not use this to verify that a group of files was copied properly — use it to verify that two disks are the same, byte for byte.

If you only have one floppy drive, you can compare two disks by typing:

```
DISKCOMP A:
```

OS/2 will prompt you to change disks.

If the two disks differ, OS/2 will display the track and side where mismatches are found.

This command will only compare two disks that are of the same type. You cannot compare high-density disks with low-density disks or 5 1/4-inch disks with 3 1/2-inch disks.

Examples: You have just copied a disk using **DISKCOPY,** but accidentally placed it next to the computer monitor. To make sure that the disk wasn't damaged by the monitor's electromagnetic fields, you could type:

```
DISKCOMP A:
```

DISKCOPY   Copies one floppy disk to another
* Protected mode
* DOS compatibility mode

Function: This command copies, byte for byte, one floppy to another.

Format: DISKCOPY [*source_drive_name*:] [*target_drive_name*:]

Comments: This command lets you copy one disk to another. Unlike **COPY** or **XCOPY**, it reads the disk byte by byte rather than file by file. You can only use **DISKCOPY** to make an exact duplicate of a floppy to another floppy of the same type. **DISKCOPY** works faster than **COPY** for disks that have many files on them. **DISKCOPY** writes over any data that was on the target disk. Because of this, you should write-protect the source disk before you copy it. If the target disk is unformatted, **DISK-COPY** will format it.

If you only have one floppy drive, you can:

```
DISKCOPY A: A:
```

OS/2 will prompt you to insert the source and target disks as necessary, and it will automatically assign a 4-byte serial number to the target disk.

If a floppy is very fragmented (see **CHKDSK**), you may want to use **XCOPY** instead of **DISK-COPY**, as **XCOPY** defragments disks.

Cancel any **SUBST** drive substitutions, **ASSIGN**, or **JOIN** commands before using **DISKCOPY**.

See also: /**S** option of **XCOPY**

Examples: Suppose you want to send a copy of a data disk to a friend. It has a lot of files in it in many subdirectories. Put a write protect tab, or set the write protect tab, on the source disk. Then place the source disk in drive A and the target disk — the one on which the copy will be made — in drive B. Type:

```
DISKCOPY A: B:
```

If you only have one drive, type:

```
DISKCOPY A: A:
```

and insert the source and target disks as prompted.

DPATH   Set a search path for data files
  * Protected mode
   DOS compatibility mode

Function: This function sets a path where OS/2 programs will look for data files.

Format: DPATH [[*drive:*] *path*] [;[*drive*]*path*] [...]

Comments: When programs look for data files, they look in the default drive and path or the particular path specified. The **DPATH** command gives a list of directories that OS/2 will search if the file is not found in the default directory.

To stop OS/2 from searching for files in the **DPATH** directories, type:

```
DPATH ;
```

To see the current **DPATH** directories, type:

```
DPATH
```

Note: Some applications, such as compilers, allow you to indicate where libraries and include files are located using the **SET** command. OS/2 looks for program files — those with CMD, COM, and EXE extensions according to the **PATH** command.

Batch files can access the **DPATH** value by looking at %DPATH%.

See also: **APPEND, PATH**

Examples: You want to use your word processor to modify the code files that are located in directories C:\BUSINESS\PROJECTS \FAILSAFE\CODE, D:\BOOK4\CODE, and A:\MISC\PASFILES. However, you don't remember which directory contains which file and would prefer not to type in such lengthy path names. You could:

```
DPATH C:\BUSINESS\PROJECTS\FAILSAFE\
 CODE; D:\BOOK4\CODE; A:\MISC\PASFILES
```

ERASE   Erase a file
  * Protected mode
  * DOS compatibility mode

Function: This command erases a file or group of files.

Format: ERASE [[*drive_name*:] [*path_name*]
                  [*file_name*]] [...]

Comments: This command is exactly the same as the **DEL** command.

See also: **DEL**

Examples: To erase all files in the current directory that
                 have a BAK or BK! extension, you could:
                 ERASE *.BAK *.BK!

EXIT   Exit a screen group
   * Protected mode
   * DOS compatibility mode
Function: This command leaves a screen group.
Format: EXIT
Comments: The Session Manager lets you start several ap-
                 plications in different screen groups. These
                 screen groups act as multitasking programs,
                 and you can easily flip between them. If you
                 want to close a screen group, you must first
                 stop any programs that are running in it. You
                 can do this by exiting your applications or hit-
                 ting Ctrl-C. Next, type **EXIT**. You will return
                 to the Session Manager.
                     In addition, you can use **COMMAND** or
                 CMD to start a secondary command proces-
                 sor, for example to give the user an OS/2 shell
                 from the middle of a program. The **EXIT** com-
                 mand returns control to the program or pre-
                 vious command processor.
See also: Chapter 4, **COMMAND, CMD**
Examples: You have just finished running an applica-
                 tion. You will no longer need this screen
                 group, so you want to free up the resources it
                 uses. Type:
                 EXIT
                     Suppose you are typing a letter in your word
                 processor. You're not wearing a watch, so you
                 want to check the time. You go to the OS/2
                 shell and type the TIME command. Having
                 done this, you want to return to the word
                 processor. You would type:
                 EXIT

FDISK　　　　　Configure or switch partition
* Protected mode
* DOS compatibility mode

Function:　　　This command switches the active partition or reconfigures the partition structure of the hard disk.

Format:　　　FDISK

Comments:　　This command is for use by advanced users only. If you have set up OS/2 and other operating systems on your hard disk, each is within its own partition. Use **FDISK** to switch to one of the other operating systems on your hard disk.

　　　　　　FDISK also sets up different partitions of the hard disk as logical drives. This means that OS/2 breaks up very large hard disks into a set of smaller disk drives, each with its own drive letter.

　　　　　　You use **FDISK** when you install a new operating system on your hard disk or to display information about the partition structure. Changing the partition structure can result in the permanent loss of any data you might already have on the hard disk.

　　　　　　Close all other screen groups when you run **FDISK**.

Examples:　　Start **FDISK** by typing **FDISK**. Select commands from the menu it displays.

FIND　　　　　Search files for text
* Protected mode
* DOS compatibility mode

Function:　　　This command searches a file or a group of files for the specified text.

Format:　　　FIND [/V] [(/C) (/N)] "*text*" [[*drive_name:*] [*path_name*] [*file_name*]] [...]

Comments:　　This command searches a file or group of files for *text*. Optionally, it will display lines in which the text isn't found, display the line numbers in which the text is found, or display the number of lines in which the text is found.

This command is very useful for finding what file contains a line of text or where a line of text is located. For example, you can search a set of program source code files for references to a particular routine or see what files mention a person named Roberta.

The text must be enclosed in quotation marks. To look for text that contains quotation marks, use two quotation marks for the single quotation mark. In other words, if you wanted to find *He said, "Hi Richard,"* you would use "He said, ""Hi Richard""" for the text string.

You cannot use wild cards in the file name.

The **/V** option instructs OS/2 to display lines that do not contain the text.

The **/C** option instructs OS/2 to indicate the number of lines that contain the text, but not to display them. When used with /V, it will count the number of lines that do not contain the text.

The **/N** option causes OS/2 to display the line number before each line that it displays.

See also: Chapter 8, for piping data into **FIND**

Examples: To search several files to display lines that mention a person named Mirna, you could type:

```
FIND "Mirna" RR.LET BAH.LET RMD.LET
 TKS.LET
```

Suppose you have a text file of orders filled for a particular month. The first column contains the name of the item sent. The rest of the line contains numbers only. To determine how many Red Banners were sent, you could:

```
FIND /C "Red Banner" ORDERS.TXT
```

FORMAT   Prepare a new disk
 * Protected mode
 * DOS compatibility mode

Function: This command prepares a new disk for use. It will also completely clear an old disk.

Format: FORMAT [*drive:*] [/4] [/T:*tracks_per_disk*]
              [/N:*sectors_per_track*] [/S] [/V[:*label*]]

Comments: The **FORMAT** command marks a disk so that OS/2 can use it. Use this command to prepare new floppies for storing data. Be very careful when you use this command — it will erase any data that was on the disk before. That is why it is best used only for disks that have never been used before. You can also use it to clear all the space used by a disk when you no longer need the data on the disk.

You can use the **FORMAT** command to format hard disks as well as floppies. This is very dangerous — you could lose all of the data on the hard disk. Only format hard disks if you are an advanced user.

FORMAT will report how many bytes are available on the disk. If portions of the disk were unusable, it will report how many bytes could not be used.

The **/S** option makes the new disk a system disk. This means that it includes the OS/2 operating system. You can then boot from the floppy. The disk must be at least 1.2M for this option to work.

The **/V** option puts a volume label on the disk. This is a line of text, up to 11 characters long, that appears whenever you **DIR** the disk. It is a useful option for keeping track of which disk is which. If you do not specify the label text OS/2 will prompt you for it.

Normally the disk is formatted according to the type of disk drive that it is in. The **/4, /T,** and **/S** options let you format low-density disks in high-density drives.

The **/4** option formats a low-density 5 1/4-inch disk (360K) in a high-density 5 1/4-inch drive (1.2M).

The **/T** option formats 3 1/2-inch disks with *tracks_per_disk* tracks on the disk. Use 80 for 720K and 1.44M disks. Note that this is an optional parameter.

The **/N** option formats 3 1/2-inch disks with *sectors_per_track* sectors on each track. Set this to 9 to format a low-density disk in a high-density 3 1/2-inch drive. (High-density 3 1/2-inch disks have 18 sectors per track.)

If you format or write to a low-density disk in a high-density drive, you might have trouble reading the disk from a low-density drive.

See also: **LABEL, VOL**

Examples: You have bought a box of new disks. So that you can store data on them at a later time, you want to format them. Type:

FORMAT A:

Insert the new disks as OS/2 prompts you. After you format each disk, put a blank disk label on it. This will let you know that the disk has been formatted.

If you want to format a disk, give it a volume name, and have it be bootable, you would:

FORMAT A: /S /V

GRAFTABL Load graphics character set
   Protected mode
 * DOS compatibility mode

Function: Loads a table of extended characters to be used on graphics screens.

Format: GRAFTABL [(*code_page*) (?) (/STA)]

Comments: In DOS compatibility mode, you can load a
              special character set for the ASCII characters
              128 to 255. The characters will work only on
              a graphics screen and are used for drawing
              and foreign language support.

              If you use the *code_page* option, use one of
              the prepared code page numbers. The **?** op-
              tion will display the choices available. The
              /STA option will display the currently loaded
              character set. If no options are given, the
              default table, which is code page 437, is
              loaded.

              Currently you can choose from:

              437   IBM U.S.
              860   Portuguese
              863   Canadian-French
              865   Nordic

              You can load a graphics character set once
              only. You may want to do that in the
              AUTOEXEC.BAT file.

See also: **CHCP**, "AUTOEXEC.BAT" section of Chapter
              10.

Examples: Suppose you want to use the Nordic charac-
              ter set with your word processor. Your word
              processor works in graphics mode. You could
              type:

              GRAFTABL 865

HELP   Explain error message
     IBM OS/2 ONLY
  * Protected mode
  * DOS compatibility mode

Function: This command explains the meaning of OS/2
              error messages. It also sets or turns off a dis-
              play message at the top of the screen that in-
              dicates whether you are in an OS/2 or DOS
              Compatibility Mode screen group.

Format: HELP [(ON) (OFF) (*message_number*)]

Comments: Entering **HELP** with no parameters displays information on returning to the Session Manager, switching between screen groups, and getting help with error messages.

        HELP ON and **HELP OFF** turn the top line display on and off. This top line indicates whether the current screen group is an OS/2 or DOS compatibility mode screen group.

        When OS/2 displays error messages, it precedes them by a seven-letter code. This code starts with DOS and ends with a four-digit number. It also gives a brief explanation of the error. If you type **HELP** followed by the four-digit number, OS/2 will display more information about the error.

        If the original message contains a file or drive name in it, the message printed by **HELP** will contain *** instead of the name.

Examples: You forget how to switch between screen groups. Type:

```
HELP
```

        You want to put a line at the top of the screen indicating whether you are in an OS/2 or DOS compatibility mode screen group. Type:

```
HELP ON
```

        You want to turn off the top line display so that there is more room on the screen when you execute OS/2 commands:

```
HELP OFF
```

        Suppose OS/2 was unable to execute one of your commands and responded with error DOS0100. To get more information on this message, you would type:

```
HELP 0100
```

or

```
HELP 100
```

HELPMSG   Explain error message
  * Protected mode
  * DOS compatibility mode

Function: This command explains the meaning of OS/2 error messages.

Format: HELPMSG *message_number*

Comments: When OS/2 displays error messages, it precedes them by a seven-letter code. This code starts with DOS and ends with a four-digit number. It also gives a brief explanation of the error. You can use HELPMSG to get more information about the error and suggestions about what might have caused the error and how to correct it. Set the *message_number* parameter to the error message's four-digit number.

If the original message contains a file or drive name in it, the message printed by HELP will contain *** instead of the name.

Examples: Suppose OS/2 was unable to execute one of your commands and responded with error DOS0100. To get more information on this message, you would type:

```
HELPMSG 0100
```
or
```
HELPMSG 100
```

JOIN   Substitutes a drive for a path
    Protected mode
  * DOS compatibility mode

Function: This command substitutes a drive for a directory name.

Format: JOIN [*drive_to_use*: *drive:directory_to_ disable*] JOIN *joined_drive_to_cancel*: /D

Comments: This function is primarily used for programs that were not designed to be used on hard disks. It allows you to change any references to a root level directory on one drive to references to another drive. For example, suppose you have a program that writes all of its temporary files in a directory called A:\TEMP. You could send these to another drive, such as a RAM drive, using the **JOIN** command.

The subdirectory that is joined must be a root level subdirectory — that is, its parent must be the root directory. Any references to the subdirectory are translated to references to the other drive. You cannot reference the other drive. Thus, you cannot set *drive_to_use* to the default drive.

Use the **/D** option to disconnect a **JOIN**. Give it the drive letter that you want to disconnect from the **JOIN**.

Typing **JOIN** with no parameters will list the set of drives and directories that are **JOIN**ed.

Remove **JOIN**S before you use the following commands: **CHKDSK, DISKCOPY, FDISK, FORMAT, LABEL, RECOVER, SYS**.

Examples: Suppose your spreadsheet saves temporary files in the A:\TEMP directory. This is slow, and forces you to keep the spreadsheet program disk in the A drive. Your D drive is a RAM drive. If you executed:

```
JOIN D: A:\TEMP
```

any further references to the A:\TEMP drive would get sent to the D: drive. Any attempts to access the D drive would fail. For example, if you did:

```
COPY \COMMAND.COM A:\TEMP
```

COMMAND.COM would get copied to the D drive. If you did:

```
COPY \COMMAND.COM D:
```

you would get an error message.

Once you had finished using your spreadsheet, you would want to disable the **JOIN**.

This would give access back to the D drive. To do this, you would:

```
JOIN D: /D
```

KEYBxx   Load keyboard layout
  * Protected mode
  * DOS compatibility mode

Function: This command replaces the U.S. keyboard layout with a different country's keyboard.

Format: KEYBxx

Comments: You can use this command to redesign the way the keyboard works. In particular, it lets you type characters that are used outside of the United States, such as the pound sign or accented vowels.

    Replace xx with one of the following codes:

Code	Country
BE	Belgium
CF	Canada (French)
DK	Denmark
FR	France
GR	Germany
IT	Italy
LA	Latin America
NL	Netherlands
NO	Norway
PO	Portugal
SF	Switzerland (French)
SG	Switzerland (German)
SP	Spain
SU	Finland
SV	Sweden
UK	United Kingdom
US	United States

    Your computer manual should detail the actual layout of the keys.

In order to use KEYB, you must first have identified the keyboard layout with the **DEVINFO** command in the CONFIG.SYS file.

See also: **DEVINFO** in "CONFIG.SYS" section of Chapter 10

Examples: Suppose you are running a program that requires you to type in the full Spanish alphabet. You have initialized the Spanish keyboard template with the **DEVINFO** command in the CONFIG.SYS file. You could enter:

KEYBSP

LABEL   Create a disk label
  * Protected mode
  * DOS compatibility mode

Function: This function creates or changes a disk's volume label.

Format: LABEL [*drive_name:*][*label_text*]

Comments: Disks can have a label that is up to 11 characters long. This label is displayed whenever the disk is **DIR**ed. The label is useful for identifying which disk is being used. You can also check the label with the **VOL** command.

If you do not supply *label_text*, OS/2 will prompt you for the text.

The label name should not include the following characters: * ? / \ | . , ; : + = < > [ ] ( ) & '

See also: **VOL, FORMAT /V** option

Examples: Suppose you store all of your personal letters to Skippy on a floppy disk. You could put a volume label on the disk by putting the disk in the A drive and typing:

LABEL A:SKIPPYLET

MKDIR or MD Make a directory or directories
* Protected mode
* DOS compatibility mode

Function: This command creates a new directory.

Format: MKDIR [[*drive_name:*][*path_name*][*new_directory_name*]] [...]

Comments: This command creates a new directory. The path name can be from the root directory or the current directory. *New_directory_name* can be any valid file name — that is, it can have an eight-character name and three-character extension composed of the same letters as can make a file name.

　　　　　　　You cannot make a directory with the same name as a file that exists in the directory's parent directory. For example, if there is a file called MIKE in the root directory, you cannot create a directory called MIKE in the root directory.

　　　　　　　In DOS compatibility mode, you can only create one directory at a time.

See also: Chapter 3, **RMDIR, CHDIR**

Examples: Suppose you want to create a directory in which you will place all of your business files. You want to put this directory in the root directory. You would type:

MKDIR \BUSINESS

or

MD \BUSINESS

　　　　　　　Suppose you now want to add a directory called INVOICES to this directory. You would type:

MD \BUSINESS\INVOICES

　　　　　　　If your current directory were the BUSINESS directory (for example, if you entered CD \BUSINESS), you would get the same result if you typed:

MD INVOICES

MODE   Set communication and output parameters
    * Protected mode
    * DOS compatibility mode

Function: This command lets you initialize parallel port, serial port, and display characteristics.

Format: MODE *display_mode* [, *number_of_lines*]
                MODE LPT*number* [*characters_per_line*]
                 [, [*lines_per_inch*][,P]]
                MODE COM*number:baud*
                 [, *parity* [,*databits* [,*stopbits*]]] [,TO = (ON) (OFF)]
                 [,XON = (ON) (OFF)]
                 [,IDSR = (ON) (OFF)]
                 [,ODSR = (ON) (OFF)]
                 [,OCTS = (ON) (OFF)]
                 [,DTR = (ON) (OFF)]
                 [,RTS = (ON) (OFF)]
                MODE COM*number*[:] *baud*
                 [,*parity* [,*databits* [, *stopbits*] [,P]]]
                MODE COM*number*

Comments: There are three major uses of the **MODE** command. It can set the characteristics of a parallel port, set the characteristics of a serial port or select a display to use.

Using MODE to select the monitor—
The most common use of **MODE** is to switch between a graphics screen and a monochrome screen on computers that have two screens. To do so, you use the:
MODE *display_mode* [, *number_of_lines*]
format, where *display_mode* is one of the following:

Display mode	Device Selected
40	40-column screen on graphics monitor
CO40	40-column screen on graphics monitor, allows color
BW40	40-column screen on graphics monitor, disables color
80	80-column screen on graphics monitor
CO80	80-column screen on graphics monitor, allows color
BW80	80-column screen on graphics monitor, disables color
MONO	Monochrome screen

The 40-column and color suppression options are for old monitors that can't adequately support color or 80 columns. (Some CGA programs use a 40-column display; most should set the mode themselves.) The most used parameters are **CO80** to select the graphics monitor and **MONO** to select the monochrome monitor.

Most display cards display 25 lines at a time. Some cards, such as the EGA card, let you display more. You can use the *number_of_lines* parameter to display more lines on the screen. Valid choices are 25, 43, and 50. The default is 25.

The other uses of mode are more complex and generally are not needed except by advanced users.

Using MODE to redirect output—
You can no longer use **MODE** to redirect output from a parallel port to a serial port. Use the **/D** and **/O** options of **SPOOL** instead.

Using MODE to configure a parallel port—
You can use **MODE** to configure a parallel printer. In general, application software will set up the printer, and you won't need to.

Use the:
```
MODE LPTnumber [ characters_per_line ]
  [, [ lines_per_inch ][ ,P ]]
```
format to configure a printer. *Number* can be 1, 2, or 3. *characters_per_line* can be 80 or 132, and *lines_per_inch* can be 6 or 8. The default values are LPT1, 80 characters per line, 6 lines per inch. You can leave a parameter unchanged by just typing a comma. The **P** option instructs OS/2 to continuously resend output to a printer if a timeout occurs.

You might want to configure the parallel printer in the AUTOEXEC.BAT or STARTUP.CMD file. Most commercial software will configure the printer for you.

Using MODE to configure a serial port
You can use **MODE** to configure a serial port. In general, application software will configure the serial port, so you won't have to.

From an OS/2 prompt, use:
```
MODE COMnumber:baud
  [, parity [ ,databits [ ,stopbits ]]]
  [ ,TO = ( ON ) ( OFF ) ] [ ,XON = ( ON
  ) ( OFF ) ][ ,IDSR = ( ON ) ( OFF ) ]
  [ ,ODSR = ( ON ) ( OFF ) ] [ ,OCTS = (
  ON ) ( OFF ) ] [ ,DTR = ( ON ) ( OFF )
  ( HS ) ] [ ,RTS = ( ON ) ( OFF ) ( HS
  ) ( TOG ) ]
```
Number can be 1 through 8. *Baud* should be the first two digits of one of the following baud rates: 110, 150, 300, 600, 1200, 2400, 4800,

9600, or 19,200. Parity can be N for none, O for odd, E for even, M for mark, or S for space. *Databits* can be 5, 6, 7 or 8; *stopbits* can be 1, 1.5, or 2. If you type only a comma, the default value is used. The default is even parity, 7 data bits, and 1 stop bit (2 stop bits for 110 baud). **TO** sets write infinite timeout processing. The default is **OFF**. **XON** sets automatic transmit flow. The default is **OFF**. **IDSR** sets data set ready input handshaking. The default is **ON**. **ODSR** sets data set ready output handshaking. The default is **ON**. **OCTS** sets clear to send output handshaking. The default is **ON**. **DTR** sets data terminal ready. The **HS** option allows data terminal ready handshaking. The default is **ON**. **RTS** sets ready to send. The **HS** option enables ready to send handshaking, and the **TOG** option enables ready to send toggling. The default is **ON**.

You can check the settings of a serial port by typing:

MODE COM*number*

This will only work in OS/2 mode.

In DOS compatibility mode use the:

MODE COM*number*[:] *baud* [,*parity*
[,*databits* [, *stopbits*] [,P]]]

format to configure a serial port. *Number* can be 1 through 8. *Baud* should be the first two digits of one of the following baud rates: 110, 150, 300, 600, 1200, 2400, 4800, 9600, or 19,200. Parity can be N for none, O for odd, or E for even. *Databits* can be 7 or 8; *stopbits* can be 1 or 2. If you type only a comma, the default value is used. The default is even parity, 7 data bits, and 1 stop bit (2 stop bits for 110 baud). The **P** option causes data to be continuously resent if there was a timeout.

You might want to configure the serial port in the AUTOEXEC.BAT or STARTUP.CMD file.

See also: Chapter 10

Examples: Suppose you have a two-screen system and you want to run a graphics program. You would type:

```
MODE CO80
```

To switch back to using your monochrome screen, you would type:

```
MODE MONO
```

MORE   Pause output every screen

   * Protected mode
   * DOS compatibility mode

Function: This command pauses an output listing every time the screen is filled.

Format: MORE < *source_file*
        source_program | MORE

Comments: Programs often output a lot of data to the screen. For example, if you use the **TYPE** command to list a file, it could fill several screens. The output won't stop, however, once it fills the screen. Instead it will whiz by, and you will probably be unable to read most of it.

The **MORE** command lets you read output one screen at a time. After a screen is filled, it pauses and displays *-more-* at the bottom of the screen. Hit Ctrl-Break to stop or any other key to continue.

You must pipe or indirect the output to **MORE**. Thus, only use **MORE** for programs that require no input from the keyboard.

See also: Chapter 8, on redirecting and piping

Examples: Suppose you want to read the text in the file README. README is quite long, though, so you want to read through it a screen at a time. You could:

```
MORE README
```

Suppose you want to run the **TREE** command. This will display a great deal of information on the screen. To read it one page at a time, you could do:

```
TREE | MORE
```

PATCH   Patch a program
  * Protected mode
  * DOS compatibility mode

Function: This command modifies particular bytes of a program file.

Format: PATCH [[*drive_name*:] [*path_name*]
        [*file_name*] [/A]

Comments: This command lets you make changes to a program's code. This command should only be used by advanced users. If you specify the **/A** option, **PATCH** will make the patches automatically after reading a special file containing patch instructions. If not, **PATCH** will prompt you for the offset of a byte to change and the new byte value, all in hexadecimal. When you are finished, **PATCH** will ask if you want to commit the changes.

Use **PATCH** with extreme caution. Make a backup copy of programs before you patch them.

Examples: The company that makes a disk utility, DISKUTIL.EXE, notifies you that it needs updating and sends you a disk with a **PATCH** instruction file. Copy this file to the directory containing the program to be **PATCH**ed and type:

```
PATCH DISKUTIL.EXE /A
```

PATH   Define search path
  * Protected mode
  * DOS compatibility mode

Function: This function defines a group of directories to search for programs not found in the current directory.

Format: PATH [[*drive_name*:][*path_name*]] [; ...]

Comments: This is an extremely useful command. When you type the name of a program to run, OS/2 looks in the current directory or the directory that you explicitly specify. This means that you need to remember what directories contain what programs. If you are working in one particular directory, you will constantly have to type long path names in order to run different programs.

                 PATH lets you get around this problem. You give it a list of directories that contain programs you plan to run. Whenever you run a program, you simply give the program name. OS/2 will search all the directories listed in **PATH** for that program.

                 The **PATH** list is limited to 128 characters. The order in which paths are listed is the order in which they are searched. Each path listed should be separated by a semicolon. To disable the **PATH** command, type:

                 PATH ;

                 To examine the current **PATH** setting type:

                 PATH

                 You should include a drive name for each path you list. Start each path from the root directory.

                 PATH differs from **DPATH** and **APPEND** in that it searches for files with BAT, CMD, COM, and EXE extensions.

                 You may want to put a **PATH** command in your AUTOEXEC.BAT and STARTUP.CMD files.

See also: **DPATH, APPEND**, Chapter 7, Chapter 10

Examples: Suppose your OS2 commands are stored in
                  the C:\OS2 directory, your word processor is
                  in the C:\WP directory, your C compiler is in
                  the C:\LANGUAGE\C directory, and various
                  utilities are in the C:\UTILITY directory. In
                  addition, you load programs that you run
                  often onto a RAM disk, which happens to be
                  the D drive. You are working in the D:\BUSI-
                  NESS\COMPPROJ directory. If you wanted to
                  use the **CHKDSK** command, you would have
                  to type C:\OS2\CHKDSK. If you wanted to
                  use your word processor, you'd have to specify
                  the C:\WP directory. This is messy. Instead,
                  you could type:

```
PATH D:;C:\OS2;C:\WP;C:\UTILITY;
 C:\LANGUAGE\C
```

Anytime you type a command name at the
prompt, OS/2 will search all of the directories
listed in the **PATH** command. For example, if
you type:

```
CHKDSK
```

OS/2 will search the current directory. As
CHKDSK is not located there, OS/2 will
search through the **PATH** directories, find
CHKDSK, and run it. You don't need to know
the directory that contains it.

The **PATH** command is especially useful
when using word processors and spreadsheets. It allows you to start these applications by simply typing their name, no matter
the directory and drive you are in.

PRINT   Print a file
  * Protected mode
  * DOS compatibility mode
Function: This command prints a file or series of files.
                  You can continue to work while the files are
                  printing.

Format: PRINT [/D:*printer_to_use*] [/B] [
            [*drive_name*:] [*path_name*] [*file_name*]] [...]
            PRINT [/D:*printer_to_use*] [(/C) (/T)]

Comments: Many applications have commands to let you
            print files. There are times, however, when
            you do not want to use an application to print
            a file. For example, there is no need to start a
            word processor to print the contents of a
            README file. Programmers often need to
            print files without using applications to do so.

            The **PRINT** command lets you print a file. It
            uses a background print queue. This means
            that you can use other programs while the file
            is printing. You can give **PRINT** several files
            to print. You don't have to wait for one to finish
            printing before you tell it to print another —
            OS/2 maintains a list of files that it needs to
            print. When it is finished with one, it moves
            to the next.

            The **PRINT** command works best for normal
            text (ASCII) files. It cannot decode spread-
            sheets, pictures, or other special files.

            You can use wild cards in the file names.
            The full name, including drive, path, and file
            name, can't be longer than 64 characters.

            The first time you **PRINT** a file, OS/2 will
            ask what device you want to use. If you just
            hit Return, LPT1 will be used. For most sys-
            tems, this is what you want.

            If you type the **PRINT** command without any
            parameters, OS/2 will display the name of the
            file being printed and the names of any files
            waiting to be printed.

            The **/D** option lets you specify a device to
            use. *printer_to_use* can be PRN, LPT1, LPT2,
            LPT3, COM1, COM2, ... COM8.

            The **/T** option cancels all files waiting to be
            printed.

The **/C** option cancels the file currently being printed.

The **/B** option causes **PRINT** to ignore end-of-file characters. This lets an entire file be printed even if it contains end-of-file marks. (This is primarily for printing data files.)

Be sure to use the **SPOOL** command if you plan to use **PRINT**. This will prevent lines from **PRINT** commands executed under different screen groups from mixing.

See also: **SPOOL**

Examples: Suppose you want to print out a README file and all C code files. You can:
```
PRINT README *.C
```

After a bit, you want to see how many files are still in the queue. Type:
```
PRINT
```

You decide that you don't want any of these printed after all. Type:
```
PRINT /T
```

PROMPT   Set system prompt
* Protected mode
* DOS compatibility mode

Function: This command sets the style of the system prompt.

Format: PROMPT [*text*]

Comments: Normally the system prompt is a set of square brackets with the current drive and directory displayed, such as [C:\]. In DOS compatibility mode, the prompt is either preceded by Real, such as [Real C:\], or is the current drive and directory followed by a greater than sign, such as C:\>. You can use the **PROMPT** command to change the prompt. For example, you can use it to display the time or date as well as the directory.

Text is the new text for the prompt. It can contain ANSI escape sequences (if ANSI is ON), normal text of the following special symbols:

Code	Result
$t	Time
$d	Date
$n	Current drive
$p	Current drive and directory
$v	OS/2 version number
$_	Carriage return — line feed
$e	Escape (ASCII 27)
$h	Backspace
$q	= character
$g	> character
$l	< character
$b	l character
$$	$ character
$c	(character
$f	) character
$a	& character
$s	space character

IBM OS/2 only:

$i	display the help line

If you change the prompt, be sure to have a different prompt for DOS compatibility mode and protected mode. You may want to set the prompt in AUTOEXEC.BAT and START-UP.CMD.

See also: Chapter 10

Examples: Suppose you want to change the prompt to your initials, the time, and the current directory. So that you have enough room to type commands, you want the time, directory name, and your initials to be on different lines. You would type:

```
PROMPT Time: $t$h$h$h $_Directory: $p
 $_[ MEG ]
```

The backspaces remove the hundredths of seconds from the time listing. The resulting prompt would look like:

```
Time: 11:04:10
Directory: C:\
[ MEG ]
```

RECOVER   Recovers files from a damaged disk
  * Protected mode
  * DOS compatibility mode

Function: This function recovers files from a damaged disk.

Format: RECOVER [*drive_name*:] [*path_name*]
         file_name
      RECOVER *drive_name*

Comments: Sometimes disk sectors go bad. This can occur after a disk is used frequently, especially if it is a low-quality disk or after some other type of damage. When a disk sector goes bad, OS/2 is unable to read it. This can have two results. If the sector was in a file, OS/2 will not be able to use the entire file. If the sector was in a directory, OS/2 will be unable to read any of the files in that directory.

There are two ways to tell if a sector has gone bad. The first is that when you try to use a file, the drive will whir or click several times, and OS/2 will print a message that it was unable to read a sector and will ask you if you want to try again. The second way to tell is if **CHKDSK** reports bad sectors on a disk that didn't have bad sectors before.

If a bad sector occurs within a text file, you can use **RECOVER** to get back most of the file.

It will read through the file and instruct OS/2 to skip over any sectors that have gone bad.[1] If the bad sector is within a program or some coded file, such as a spreadsheet, **RECOVER** cannot help you. It will alter the file so that you can access the data that wasn't bad, but the file will most likely be unusable. Never run a program file that you have **RECOVER**ed.

If the bad sector occurs within a directory, you will be unable to access any of the files within that directory. In this case, you should first copy from the disk all of the files that aren't in the directory. After you have made a backup of these good files, erase them from the bad disk. Then, run **RECOVER** on the whole disk. **RECOVER** will look through the disk and put together all of the files. Unfortunately, since the directory was damaged, it doesn't know the file names. Thus, it gives them all numeric names. You need to go through and rename each of the files in the recovered directory, using the original names. This can be quite difficult, especially if the disk contains many files or if the bad directory had many directories under it.[2]

RECOVER is best used by advanced users. If you have a disk that goes bad, see if you can find an advanced user to help you. There are many methods less drastic than **RECOVER**

---

[1] It removes a cluster from the file chain and marks the File Allocation Table (FAT) entry as bad.

[2] **RECOVER** completely ignores the entire disk directory structure. It scans the FAT for file chains and gives them new root directory entries with a unique numeric file name. Some of these files will be directories. You will need a sector editor to restore their status as directories. You will also need to rename and repoint the subdirectories and files. By backing up and erasing the good files, a minimum number of chains will be left in the FAT. If you did not erase the good files, they too would be given a numeric name.

that the advanced user can employ to recover bad disks and files.

Examples:

A text file on your floppy, NEWSLET.TXT, has gone bad. You want to use **RECOVER** to get back as much of it as possible. You could:

```
RECOVER A:NEWSLET.TXT
```

When you try to **DIR** the \PERSONAL directory of a floppy, the drive whirs and clicks, and then you get an OS/2 error message indicating a bad sector. You should:

1): Try using that directory from another disk drive. If you can read it from another drive, make a backup copy using that drive.

2): If it is a 5 1/4-inch disk, hold the disk lightly by the outside. Put your fingers into the big hole in the middle and rotate it until you can see through the little hole to the right of the big hole. Try reading the disk again.

3): Get someone else to try.

4): Try to find an advanced user to help you.

5): Use **XCOPY** to back up as many files as possible. Be sure to copy these files to some good floppies. Erase *from the damaged disk* all of the files that you could back up. Do not erase these files from the backup disks. Then, type:

```
RECOVER A:
```

When RECOVER is finished, you will need to figure out which files were which. Good luck! An advanced user with a sector editor would be of help.

If **RECOVER** indicates that not all the files were recovered because it ran out of directory space, copy all of the recovered files to a floppy disk. Then erase the files from the damaged disk and run **RECOVER** again.

After you have restored the names of as many files as possible, recreate the disk using the backup of the good files and the recovered files from the bad directory. Do not recreate the disk on the damaged disk — use a new disk. While OS/2 knows not to use the bad sectors on a damaged disk, the disk is not trustworthy. Throw it out or give it to someone you don't like.

6): Scream and curse.

RENAME or REN Rename a file
  * Protected mode
  * DOS compatibility mode

Function: This command renames a file or group of files.

Format: RENAME [*drive_name*:] [*directory_name*] *original_name new_name*

REN [*drive_name*:] [*directory_name*] *original_name new_name*

Comments: This command changes the name of a file or group of files. It is useful for reorganizing directories. You can also use it to more easily copy files. You can use wild cards in the file name.

Examples: Suppose you want to rename a file that is called C:\PEANUTS\GOOBER.TXT to GOOBER.OLD. You might do this because you plan to create another file called GOOBER.TXT and you want a backup of the original version. You would type:
```
REN C:\PEANUTS\GOOBER.TXT GOOBER.OLD
```

Suppose you are writing a book that has several sections for Chapter 7. All of these files start with the letters CHAP7. You want to make them Chapter 8 files instead. You could:
```
REN CHAP7*.* CHAP8*.*
```

REPLACE   Replace files
  * Protected mode
  * DOS compatibility mode

Function: This command lets you replace files in one directory with files of the same name from another directory.

Format: REPLACE [*source_drive:*] [*source_path*]
      [*source_file*] [*target_drive:*] [*target_path*]
      [(/S) (/A)] [/P] [/R] [/W]

Comments: This command is useful for updating versions of software. It lets you copy all files from one directory to another as long as a file with the same name already exists on the directory. For example, suppose you have taken some files home from work. You place them on a disk with personal letters as well. At home, you modify some of the files for your job. When you get to the office the next day, you can quickly copy all of the job-related files that you have updated, without your personal letters being copied as well.

You can also instruct **REPLACE** to copy files only if they don't already exist. This is useful for copying new files to a directory when you don't want files that already exist to be modified.

You can use wild cards in the source file name. If you omit it, the whole directory is used.

The **/S** flag causes all subdirectories of the target directory to be searched for matching files.

The **/A** flag copies files only if files with that name do not already exist in the target directory.

The **/P** flag asks if you want to replace a file before each replacement is made.

The **/R** file replaces read-only files as well as writable files.

The **/W** option prompts you to insert a disk before the replacing begins.

Examples: You have copied files from several directories in the BUSINESS directory so that you can work on them at home. When you get back to the office, you want to update the files on the office computer. Instead of copying each file to its respective directory — which would take time and require you to remember the source directory — you can:

```
REPLACE A:\*.*  C:\BUSINESS /S
```

Suppose that you have taken home some letters to summarize. You create new files containing the summaries, and you also put your own comments inside the letters. Naturally, you don't want the rest of the office to be able to read your comments. To just copy the summary files, you could:

```
REPLACE A:\*.* C:\BUSINESS /A
```

RESTORE   Restore backed-up files
   * Protected mode
   * DOS compatibility mode

Function: This command lets you restore files to a disk from a backup disk.

Format: RESTORE *back_up_drive*: [*target_drive*] [*target_path*] [*target_file*] [/S] [/P] [/B: *date*] [/A: *date*] [/E: *time*] [/L: *time*] [/M] [/N]

Comments: You should back up your hard disks regularly. If something should happen to your hard disk, you can use **RESTORE** to bring back files that you have backed up with the **BACK-UP** command. You can restore single files, groups of files, or all the files on the disk.

You can use wild cards in the target file name.

The **/S** option restores all files in subdirectories of the directory.

The **/P** option instructs OS/2 to ask for permission before restoring read-only files or files that have changed since the last backup.

The **/B** option causes files to be restored only if they were modified before or on *date*.

The **/A** option causes files to be restored only if they were modified after or on *date*.

The **/E** option restores files only if the target files were modified at or earlier than *time*.

The **/L** option restores files only if the target files were modified at or after *time*.

The **/M** option restores files only if the target files were modified after the last backup.

The **/N** option restores files only if they no longer exist on the target disk.

See also: **BACKUP**

Examples: You used **BACKUP** to back up a directory called \PRESMANG\APPCODE. You accidentally erased most of the files from this directory. To get them back, you could put the back-up disk in drive A and type:

RESTORE A: C:\PRESMANG\APPCODE /N

RMDIR or RD Remove directories
  * Protected mode
  * DOS compatibility mode

Function: This command removes a directory structure or group of directory structures.

Format: RMDIR [[*drive:*] [*path*]] [...]
                 RD [[*drive:*] [*path*]] [...]

Comments: This command removes a directory or a group of directories. It is useful for cleaning up a disk's directory structure. Only remove a directory when you no longer need to use it.

Directories must be empty before they can be removed.

You cannot remove the default directory. In DOS Compatibility Mode, you can only remove one directory at a time.

See also: Chapter 3

Examples: It is the end of the year, and you no longer need any of the files in the \CLIENTS\JOEV, \CLIENTS\TERRYL, and \CLIENTS\PETEM directories. You have already made backups of the files in these directories and erased the files from the hard disk. You could then:

```
RMDIR \CLIENTS\JOEV \CLIENTS\TERRYL \
  CLIENTS\PETEM
```

You could also use **RD** instead of **RMDIR**. Another option would be to:

```
CD \CLIENTS
RD JOEV TERRYL PETEM
```

Note that in DOS compatibility mode you would need to enter three separate **RMDIR** commands

SET   Set environment value

  * Protected mode

  * DOS compatibility mode

Function: This command equates a value to a variable in the environment.

Format: SET [*var_name* = [*var_value*]]

Comments: This command is used primarily by advanced users. The environment is an area of memory in which OS/2 stores information, such as what the prompt is and what the **PATH** search path is. You can use the environment to pass information to programs or batch files.

Typically, the environment is used to tell a program where certain files, such as compiler libraries, are located. Application software that requires environment variables to be set will usually detail how to set them.

If you don't include any parameters, OS/2 will display all values in the environment. If you don't provide a variable value, OS/2 will remove the variable definition from the environment.

If you do include parameters, be sure that there is no space between the name, the equal sign, and the parameters.

Each screen group has its own environment.

You can access any of the values set by **SET** at the OS/2 prompt or from batch files. Precede and follow the variable name by percent signs. For example, %PATH% will be substituted by the current value of the **PATH** command. You can use %PATH%, %DPATH%, %PROMPT%, %COMSPEC%, or any user-defined variables.

As mentioned, you can access these values from the OS/2 prompt. This is very useful. For example, suppose you want to add a new directory to the list of **INCLUDE** directories. Instead of retyping in the old directory name and adding in the new directory, you can just:

```
SET INCLUDE=%INCLUDE%;C:\NEWDIR
```

See also: Chapter 7, Chapter 9, Chapter 10

Examples: Suppose your compiler determines the location of library files by checking the **LIB** setting in the environment. You have stored the libraries in the root directory of the E drive and in the C:\LANGUAGES\C\LIB directory. To tell the compiler this, you would type:

```
SET LIB=E:\;C:\LANGUAGE\C\LIB
```

You also need to use some special libraries stored in the C:\LANGUAGE\REALIZER\LIB directory. You could:

```
SET LIB=%LIB%;C:\LANGUAGE\REALIZER\LIB
```

SETCOM40   Allow serial device use in DOS compatibility mode

IBM OS/2 Only

   Protected mode

*   DOS compatibility mode

Function: This command allows DOS programs that use a modem, serial printer, plotter, or mouse to operate in the DOS Compatibility Mode.

Format: SETCOM40 COM*number* = (ON) (OFF)

Comments: Programs written for the DOS environment that use serial ports might have difficulty running in the DOS Compatibility Mode of OS/2. In particular, they will not be able to find the port address of a device attached to a serial port. The SETCOM40 command allows them to do so. You will need to execute this command before you run communications (modem) programs in the DOS compatibility mode.

   Number indicates the number of the serial port. It can be 1, 2, or 3. The port must have been initialized with a DEVICE=COM0*x*.SYS statement in the CONFIG.SYS file. Using the **ON** option allows the port to be found; using the **OFF** option disables it.

   Set the serial port **ON** before you start the DOS program that needs serial ports. Set it **OFF** when you are finished.

   If a program in an OS/2 screen group is using a serial port for output, don't use the same serial port in the DOS Compatibility Mode screen group until the program in the OS/2 screen group is finished. This will prevent overwrite errors.

See also: COM0*x*.SYS driver in Chapter 10.

Examples: You are about to run a DOS communications
program so that you can log on to a bulletin
board. First make sure that there aren't any
communications programs running in other
screen groups. Then switch to the DOS compatibility mode screen group and type:
SETCOM40 COM1 = ON
When your program finishes, you type:
SETCOM40 COM1 = OFF

SORT   Sort a file
  * Protected mode
  * DOS compatibility mode
Function: This command sorts a file.
Format: *program* | SORT [/R] [/+*start_col*]
SORT [/R] [/+*start_col*] *file_name*
Comments: This command is useful for sorting files. It is
always used with indirection or piping. Its
output can also be directed or piped. Refer to
Chapter 8 for more details on redirection and
piping.
    The file is sorted line by line, and the result
is displayed on the screen. Upper- and lower-
case letters are not distinguished.
    The **/R** option causes the file to be sorted in
reverse alphabetical order.
    The **/+** option starts the comparison with
the *start_col* character of each line.
See also: Chapter 8
Examples: Suppose you want to sort the names of the
files on the E drive according to their extension. You could:
DIR E: |SORT /+10

SPOOL   Enable print spooling
  * Protected mode
  * DOS compatibility mode

Function: This command allows application printouts to be spooled by setting up a print buffer.

Format: SPOOL [*drive_name:*] [*directory_name*]
                 [/D:*device*] [/O: *device*]

Comments: This is a very useful feature. Applications often print lengthy files. For many programs, the user must wait until printing is finished before continuing working. The **SPOOL** command lets you continue to work while documents are being printed. Documents from different screen groups are spooled. New jobs start on new pages.

                 The **SPOOL** command differs from the **PRINT** command in that **SPOOL** spools output from programs. **PRINT** prints particular files in the background.

                 The drive and directory specify where temporary information will be stored by **SPOOL**.

                 Because a system could contain many printers, applications may access each of these printers. The printers are named PRN, LPT1, LPT2, and LPT3. You need to set up a separate spooler for each printer. The **/D** option specifies which printer the spooler will act for. Set *device* to PRN, LPT1, LPT2, or LPT3.

                 The **/O** option names the actual output print device. You can use this to redirect output from a parallel printer to a serial printer. In other words, suppose you only have a serial printer, but all of your software accesses LPT1. By using the **/O** option, you can send all output intended for LPT1 to a serial printer. Set *device* to LPT1, LPT2, LPT3, PRN, COM1, COM2, or COM3. The default is the device specified by the **/D** option.

                 If you use the **/O** option to redirect output to a serial printer, be sure that the serial port parameters are those that the printer expects. You may need to use the **MODE** command first to change the serial port parameters.

Programs running in DOS compatibility mode might not print out pages sent to the spooler until the programs stops. To force printer output in DOS compatibility mode, press Ctrl-Alt-Prt Sc.

If you have used the **PRINT** command, be sure that the queue is empty before starting **SPOOL**. You can ensure this by typing:

```
PRINT /T
```

It is a good idea to start the spooler before you use the **PRINT** command.

You may want to start the spooler automatically in the CONFIG.SYS file.

See also:	**PRINT**
Examples:	Suppose you are running a scientific package that prints long files. You are often prevented from continuing to work while you wait for the printing to finish. You could solve this problem by typing:

```
SPOOL
```

Your programs always write to LPT1, but the printer you normally use there is broken. You do, however, have a printer attached to COM2. You can use this for output by typing:

```
SPOOL /D:LPT1 /O:COM2
```

START   Start an OS/2 program in a new screen group
  *   Protected mode
     DOS compatibility mode

Function:	This command starts a new OS/2 screen group and runs a program in it.
Format:	START ["*program_title*"] [/C] *program_name* [*program_parameters*]
Comments:	You can use this command to automatically start up screen groups and programs from

batch files. In particular, it is useful for automatically starting up programs when the OS/2 is booted.

The *program_title* is the name that will appear in the Session Manager's **Running Program** list. The default is the name of the program.

The /C option instructs OS/2 to end the screen group after the program finishes. Use this option when you use **START** to automatically start up word processors and other such applications. For screen groups running OS/2 commands, you may or may not want to use this option.

Program_name is the name of the program to run. It can be an application program or an OS/2 command.

Program_parameters are any extra parameters you want to pass to the program.

If you want to redirect the output of a program that is started with **START**, you must enclose the program name and redirection within double quotes. You also must specify a program title.

See also: **RUN** in Chapter 10

Examples: You want your word processor to automatically start up when you turn on the computer. The word processor is called WP and is located in the C:\WP directory. You could add the following line to the STARTUP.CMD file:

```
START "Word Processor" /C C:\WP
```

You want to make a batch file to start your spreadsheet with the payroll file and also make a hard copy of the names of all the files in the PAYROLL directory. You could use the following lines:

```
START "Spread Sheet-Payroll" /C
  C:\SPRDSHT\PL C:\PAYROLL\PAYROLL.PLS
```

```
START "Print file names" "DIR
  C:\PAYROLL PRN"
```

SUBST   Substitute a drive for a path
    Protected mode
  * DOS compatibility mode

Function: This command substitutes a drive name for a path.

Format: SUBST [*new_drive*: *real_drive*:*real_directory*]
                  SUBST *drive*:[*directory*] /D

Comments: This command allows references to drive letters to replace a path. For example, **SUBST** could be used to make all references to the H drive mean "use the C:\LANGUAGE\C directory." **SUBST** is useful for old-style DOS programs that don't recognize directories and as a shortcut to typing long path names.

                  The *new_drive* parameter must be a drive that doesn't exist.

                  If you use **SUBST** without parameters, current substitutions are printed.

                  The **/D** option removes substitution for a particular drive.

See also: **ASSIGN**

Examples: Suppose you are tired of typing C:\BOOKS\WINDOWS\TEXT whenever you want to edit chapters for a book on Microsoft Windows. You could type:
```
SUBST W: C:\BOOKS\WINDOWS\TEXT
```
                  If you were to type DIR W:, you would see a listing of all the files in the C:\BOOKS\WINDOWS\TEXT directory.

                  Once you were finished, you could remove the link by typing:
```
SUBST W: /D
```

SYS   Make system disk
  * Protected mode
  * DOS compatibility mode

Function: This command creates an OS/2 system disk
                 by copying the OS/2 system files.

Format: SYS *drive*:

Comments: This command creates an OS/2 system disk.
                 This allows the disk to be booted. The disk
                 must be formatted and empty.

                   After using SYS, you should copy COM-
                 MAND.COM and CMD.EXE to the target drive.

Examples: Suppose you want to make the floppy in drive
                 A a system disk. It is formatted and empty.
                 You would type:
                 SYS A:

TIME   Check or change the time
  * Protected mode
  * DOS compatibility mode

Function: This command sets or changes the system
                 time.

Format: TIME [*hours*:*minutes*[:*seconds*[.*hundredths*]]]

Comments: This command lets you check or set the sys-
                 tem time. If you type **TIME** without
                 parameters, OS/2 will display the time and
                 ask if you want to change it. If you hit Enter,
                 the system time will not be altered. If you
                 change the time, enter the time in 24-hour for-
                 mat.

                   This command sets the internal clock.

                   If you are using a non-U.S. time format, you
                 may have to enter the time in a different for-
                 mat.

See also: **COUNTRY** command in "CONFIG.SYS" sec-
                 tion of Chapter 10

Examples: You want to see what time it is. Type:
                 TIME

When asked if you want to change the time, simply hit Return.

TREE   Display disk structure
  * Protected mode
  * DOS compatibility mode

Function: This command displays the directory struc-ture of the disk.

Format: TREE [*drive:*] [/F]

Comments: This command is very useful if you want to review how you have set up the directory structure on a disk.

     If you use the **/F** option, all the files in each directory will be listed when the directory structure is displayed.

See also: Chapter 3

Examples: Suppose you want to see how you have or-ganized the directory structure on your hard disk. You could type:

    TREE C:

     Because the listing will be long, you might want to send the output to the **MORE** com-mand:

    TREE C: | MORE

TYPE   Type a file
  * Protected mode
  * DOS compatibility mode

Function: This command types out a file or files.

Format: TYPE [[*drive_name:*]
         [*directory_name*][*file_name*]] [...]

Comments: This command is useful for listing the con-tents of a file. It works best with normal text (ASCII) files; programs and binary files will print garbage.

     You might want to direct the output to the printer or the **MORE** command.

In DOS compatibility mode, you can only list one file at a time. In OS/2 screen groups, you can **TYPE** multiple files and use wild cards.

Examples: Suppose you want to see what is in the README file on the A drive. You could type:
```
TYPE A:README
```
If it flashed by too quickly, you could type:
```
TYPE A:README | MORE
```
To print the file, you could:
```
TYPE A:README > PRN
```

VER   Display OS/2 version
  * Protected mode
  * DOS compatibility mode

Function: This command displays the OS/2 version number.

Format: VER

Comments: Some programs may require later versions of OS/2 in order to run.

Examples: You want to see the OS/2 version that you are using. Type:
```
VER
```

VERIFY   Set verify status
  * Protected mode
  * DOS compatibility mode

Function: This command selects the verify status. This determines whether OS/2 verifies that data is written correctly as it writes.

Format: VERIFY [(ON) (OFF)]

Comments: In most cases OS/2 has no problems writing files. Sometimes, however, an error could occur, especially if a disk is in bad condition. Setting **VERIFY** mode on instructs OS/2 to confirm that all data is written correctly. This slows down writing.

Use the **ON** option to set **VERIFY** mode on and the **OFF** option to turn it off. Typing

VERIFY with no parameters prints the current verify status.

Examples: You are about to copy a crucial file to a floppy. You are a little worried that the data will not be copied correctly. You could type:

VERIFY ON

VOL   Print volume name
*   Protected mode
*   DOS compatibility mode

Function: This command prints a disk's volume label.

Format: VOL [*drive_name*:] [...]

Comments: You can put a label of up to 11 characters on a disk using the **LABEL** or **FORMAT /V** command. This volume is displayed every time you **DIR** the disk and is useful for identifying the disk. The **VOL** command also causes the disk label to be displayed.

In DOS compatibility mode you can only examine the label of one disk at a time.

See also: **LABEL, FORMAT /V** option

Examples: Suppose you want to determine the volume labels of the disks in the A and B drives. You could:

VOL A: B:

XCOPY   Copy files and subdirectories
*   Protected mode
*   DOS compatibility mode

Function: This command is an extended file copier.

Format: XCOPY [*source_drive*:] [*source_path*]
               [*source_file*] [*dest_drive*:] [*dest_path*]
               [*dest_file*] [/S [/ E]] [/P] [/V] [(/A)
               (/M)] [/D:*date*]

Comments: This is a very powerful copy command. It allows you to copy a whole disk or directory, including any directories under it. It also allows you to copy files created after a certain date. This is a very useful command for copying files and for making backups. It is also useful for defragmentizing a disk.

You can use wild cards in the file names.

The **/S** option instructs **XCOPY** to copy any non-empty subdirectories.

The **/E** option instructs **XCOPY** to also copy any empty subdirectories. It must be used with the **/S** option.

The **/P** option instructs **XCOPY** to prompt you before it copies each file.

The **/V** option causes **XCOPY** to verify that each file was written without errors.

The **/A** option instructs **XCOPY** to copy only files whose archive bit is set.

The **/M** option instructs **XCOPY** to copy only files whose archive bit is set, and to clear the archive bit after copying the file.

The **/D** option instructs **XCOPY** to copy only files modified on or after *date*. The format of *date* depends upon the **COUNTRY** setting. For the United States, it is mm-dd-yy

See also: **COPY**

Examples: Suppose you want to copy all files in the ADVDOSGD directory to a floppy. This directory also has files within a subdirectory. You would:

```
XCOPY ADVDOSGD A: /S
```

Suppose that you copied some computer program files to a RAM disk. You made a series of changes to some of them and wrote a few new ones. You want to copy the new and the modified files to the hard disk, but you don't want to copy old files or any of the other files on the RAM disk. Assuming the data is 9-19-87, you could:

```
XCOPY D:\*.* C:\PROGRAMS\*.* /D:9-19-87
```

You have used the disk in drive A fairly frequently, and **CHKDSK** reports that it is quite
fragmented. This slows down the speed with
which you can access it. You could place an
empty floppy in drive B and type:
```
XCOPY A:\*.*   B:\ /S
```
The floppy in the B drive will have all of the
files from the floppy in the A drive, but they
will not be fragmented.

7

Tips on Using Commands

This chapter presents a few tips that will help you get the most out of OS/2 commands.

Using PATH and DPATH

The **PATH** and **DPATH** commands will save you a great deal of time. Look over your hard disk and find the directories that contain programs you frequently use. In particular, look for directories, such as /OS2, that contain OS/2 commands or utilities. Note which directories contain your word processor, spreadsheet, and database. If you are a programmer, jot down directories that contain your compilers. If you have a RAM disk, note its letter, too. You should place the names of all of these directories in the **PATH** statement. That way OS/2 can automatically find programs for you. When you type a program name, OS/2 will look in the current directory and all of the **PATH** directories until it finds it. You don't need to type in the full drive and path name. Order the directory names in terms of which are more frequently used. Always put any RAM drive directories first — they are the quickest for OS/2 to search.

For example, most OS/2 commands are in \OS2. Suppose your utilities are in \UTILITY, your word processor in \WP, your spreadsheet in \MP, your database in \DB, and your C compiler in \LANGUAGE\C. In addition, the D and E drives are RAM disks. You would type:

```
PATH D:;E:;C:\OS2;C:\UTILITY;C:\WP;C:\MP;C:\DB;C:
\LANGUAGE\C
```

Though you can type this command at the prompt, you should put it in the AUTOEXEC.BAT and OS2INIT.CMD files.

The **DPATH** command is similar to **PATH**, only it tells OS/2 what directories to search through for data files. It is most useful for indicating where help files and other such information are located. Though you can also use it to create a list of directories that will be searched for data files, such as spreadsheets, this can add confusion to the way you interact with your directory structure.

You can modify **PATH** and **DPATH** entries without retyping in the old entry. Use %PATH% to represent the old **PATH** value and %DPATH% to represent the old **DPATH** value. For example, suppose you want to add the D:\WP directory to the **PATH** statement. You could:

```
PATH %PATH%;D:\WP
```

Copying Files

When you need to copy files, strongly consider using the **XCOPY** command. It lets you copy directories and all nested directories as well. **XCOPY** is also useful when you want to just copy files that you modified after a certain date. For example, if you are a programmer, you probably copy all of your source code to a RAM disk to speed compilation time. You can use **XCOPY** to copy all the files you have changed to your hard disk or to a floppy.

You can also use **XCOPY** to make backups of files that have changed recently. To do so, use the **/A** option. It will only copy files that haven't been backed up.

Quickly Creating Disk Files

There are many times when you need to create a very short text disk file. For example, you might want to make a brief README file for a user, make a quick batch file, or type a brief letter. If you don't have an editor handy or don't want to bother starting one, you can redirect all keyboard input into a file. To do this, type:

```
COPY CON: file_name
```

then begin typing the file. When you are finished, hit the F6 key or Ctrl-Z. The file will be written.

Printing Results of OS/2 Commands

Many times it is useful to have printouts of what appears on the screen. For example, you might like to print out the result of a **DIR** command or a **TREE** command. You can do this by following the command with a > *PRN*. This instructs OS/2 to send the output to the printer. For example, if you wanted to have a printout of all files in a directory, you could type:

```
DIR > PRN
```

If you wanted to print a file that you have sorted with **SORT**, you could use:

```
SORT < filename > PRN
```

If you want to print several files in a row, each on a separate page, you will need to make a special file that instructs the printer to start a new page. To do this, make a short file containing the form-feed character. Type:

```
COPY CON: FF
```

Then hit Ctrl-L and Ctrl-Z. Every time you want a new page to start, type:

```
COPY FF PRN:
```

You can also use **FF** to force the last page in a laser printer to be printed, instead of having to take the printer off line and hit the form-feed button.

Speeding Access with RAM Disks

Many programs need to use temporary disk files. You can speed time greatly by instructing the programs to put temporary files on any RAM disks that you have set up. If your applications have an option for selecting the temporary drive, give them the letter of your RAM disk.

Many programs also check the environment for a TEMP or TMP setting to determine what drive to use for RAM disks. Set this to the letter of your RAM disk. For example, if your D drive is a RAM disk, you could type:

```
SET TEMP=D:
```

Running DOS Programs

You should be able to run most DOS programs in the DOS compatibility mode. If you are running communications programs or programs using a serial printer, be sure to use the **SETCOM40** command. You may want to create an

AUTOEXEC.BAT file to initialize the DOS mode (see Chapters 9 and 10). If your programs absolutely do not work, put the DOS boot disk in drive A and reboot the computer. Then run the programs.

Summary

- Use the **PATH** and **DPATH** commands so that OS/2 can automatically find the locations of files without you specifically directing it.
- You can append to **PATH** and **DPATH** values by using **SET** and %PATH% or %DPATH% instead of retyping in the value.
- **XCOPY** is a powerful copy command. It lets you copy files as well as directories.
- You can create small text files by using **COPY CON**:
- You can print the results of programs by using **> PRN**. This is very useful for getting a hard copy of a directory listing. To force separation of pages, create and send the **FF** file.
- RAM disks can speed programs that have heavy disk access.

8

Redirection, Piping, and Grouping

In this chapter you'll learn how to use redirection, piping, and grouping. Redirecting and piping let you use alternate input and output and chain together programs to greatly enhance OS/2 features. Grouping lets you combine several OS/2 commands together in powerful ways.

Redirection

Redirection lets you change where a file sends its output and where it gets its input. This lets you easily save the results of commands to files or have the results printed. You can also have a program take its input from a disk file instead of the keyboard, making it run without user intervention.

Normally programs send their output to the screen. For example, when you type **DIR**, a listing of all files in the directory appears on the screen. Sometimes it would be more useful to have this information saved in a file or printed on the printer. You can do this with *outdirection*. Outdirection instructs OS/2 to send output intended for the screen to another device. To use outdirection, you follow a program's name with:

```
> device
```

or

```
> file
```

For example, suppose you want to print out the results of the **DIR** command. You could type:

```
DIR C:\*.DOC > PRN
```

The **> PRN** instructs DOS to take the results of the **DIR** command and send them to the printer. Note that the **> PRN** occurs after all of the **DIR** parameters.

If you wanted to save the results of a **DIR** command to a file, you could:

```
DIR C:\PAYROLL\*.CHK   > A:\CHECK.LST
```

This instructs OS/2 to list all files in the PAYROLL directory that have the CHK extension and to save the results in a file called CHECK.LST in the root directory of the A drive. You could then print this file or load it into a word processor.

Outdirection works only with programs that have text output. Programs with graphics, special manipulation of the screen, and so forth do not work well with outdirection. In addition, avoid using outdirection with programs that ask for input. The prompts for input will be outdirected as well! You'll have to guess as to what the program is asking.

Some programs take all of their input from the keyboard. Many times you want to repeat a lengthy series of inputs over and over. For example, you might be testing a program and always type in the same list of stock prices. Or, there might be a few scenarios that you frequently run over and over. *Indirection* lets you use a file as input instead of the keyboard. Indicate indirection with the < sign:

```
< file_name
```

For example, suppose you have a program that reads names and addresses and then prints out mailing labels. It asks for the number of people on the list and then prompts for the rest of the information. You could type in all the information each time you wanted to print your mailing list. Most likely, though, you will add names every now and then and not completely throw out a list after you have used it. You could create a file that had the number of names in it, followed by the names and addresses of everyone on the list. You could then run this into the mailing label program:

```
MAILLBLS < MAIL.LST
```

By editing the file, you could easily change the labels.

You can use indirection and outdirection together. For example, the following command sorts a file and saves the result in a new file:

```
SORT < INPUT.FIL > SORTED.FIL
```

Instead of outdirecting results, you can also **APPEND** results. The **APPEND** command, >>, redirects the output, but instead of creating a brand-new file, it adds the information to the end of an existing file. (If the named file doesn't exist, OS/2 will create it.) **APPEND**'s format is:

```
> file_name
```

For example, suppose you have a program called TIMESTMP that prints out the time and date. You use this program to keep track of when you start and stop working on the computer. Each time you start or stop work, you could type:

```
TIMESTMP >> TIMELOG.TXT
```

The file TIMELOG.TXT will contain a list of all the start and stop times.

OS/2 also has predefined files that you can use for redirection:

File	Meaning
0	Standard input
1	Standard output
2	Standard error

For example, suppose you wanted to send all error messages from an OS/2 command to a file. You could:

```
DIR *.*  > PRN 2> ERRFILE
```

Do not put blanks between the 0, 1, or 2 and the >or< sign.

Piping

Piping is very similar to redirection. Piping lets you take the output from one program and use it as the input to another program. Piping is indicated by the I symbol.

For example, suppose you want to sort the directory listing of a disk and print the result on the printer. You could:

```
DIR C:  | SORT > PRN
```

The results of the **DIR** command are used as the input for the **SORT** command. The results of the **SORT** command are sent to the printer.

Note that:

```
DIR C: | SORT
```

is the same as:

```
DIR C: > TEMP.FIL
```

```
SORT < TEMP.FIL
```

You can string several pipes together. For example, suppose you want a sorted listing of all directories in the current and root directories and the E drive. You could:

```
DIR *.* \*.* E:*.* | FIND "<DIR> " | SORT > PRN
```

This command first lists all files in the current, root, and E drive. It sends the result to the **FIND** command. **FIND** pulls out all lines that are directories. **SORT** sorts these directories and sends them to the printer.

Grouping

Grouping is a very powerful technique. It lets you run several OS/2 commands at the same time. You can use the results of one command to determine whether to run another. Grouping does not work in DOS Compatibility Mode.

There are three main grouping operations: **ALL, AND**, and **OR**. The **ALL** command lets you execute a list of OS/2 commands. The & character indicates the **ALL** command. Place it between a list of commands to execute. Each will be run in left-to-right order.

For example, suppose you want to print out a sorted directory listing. However, you want to use the **PRINT** command so that the results will be spooled. You could type:

```
DIR | SORT > TEMP.FIL & PRINT TEMP.FIL
```

The **AND** command, indicated by &&, performs one OS/2 command. If that command is successful, it performs the next command. For example, suppose you want to copy all of the files in a directory to a new location. You then want to erase and remove the original directory. Of course, you don't want to erase the files if the copy wasn't successful. You could:

```
MD \MIRNA && COPY \LETTERS\MIRNA \MIRNA && DEL
    \LETTERS\MIRNA && RD \LETTERS\MIRNA
```

The **OR** command, | |, performs either the command on the left or the command on the right. OS/2 starts by trying the command on the left. If that works, OS/2 stops. If not, OS/2 does the command on the right. For example, suppose you want to either run a program to select the laser printer, called SETLASER, or one to select a dot matrix printer, called SET-DOTMT. You don't want to run both programs. You could type:

```
SETLASER || SETDOTMT
```

You can combine &, &&, and | | on the same line. You can also enclose groups of commands within parentheses to order them. For example, you could:

```
(SETLASER || SETDOTMT) && (TYPE BARBARA.LET
    DAVE.LET & SORT < DIR > PRN) || COPY CON:
    GREENE.LET
```

Summary

- Outdirection lets you send output normally displayed on the screen to a file or to a device, such as a printer.
- Indirection lets you use a file instead of the keyboard as input to a program.

- Piping lets you use the output of one program as the input to another.
- Grouping commands lets you execute a series of OS/2 commands on one line. You can alter what commands run according to the success of other commands.

9

Batch Files

Batch files are OS/2 utilities that you can easily build. They are composed of normal OS/2 commands and a few useful programming structures. In this chapter you'll learn how to make batch files. Chapter 12 contains some powerful batch file utilities that you can type in and use.

Simple Batch Files

There are many OS/2 commands that you will run over and over. For example, you might want to set **PATH** and **DPATH** every time you start a new screen group. Or, you might frequently copy the same files to a RAM disk or back up certain directories before you go home. Instead of typing these commands over and over, you can put them into a batch file. When you type the name of the batch file, all of the commands in it run. For example, suppose your batch file contained the following lines:

```
DIR A:\HOMECOPY\*.LET > PRN
COPY A:\HOMECOPY\*.LET D:\BUSINESS\LETTERS && ERASE
 A:\HOMECOPY\*.LET
WP
```

When you run the batch file, OS/2 will print the names of all letter files in the A:\HOMECOPY directory. It will then copy the letter files to the BUSINESS LETTERS directory and erase all of the letters from the A disk. Then, it will start the word processor. You could run such a program after bringing business letters that you worked on at home to the office.

While the previous example might not be of use to you, there are many times when batch files will be useful to you. You will find several useful ones in Chapter 12. Besides their use as utilities, batch files give you a shortcut to executing commands. You can also use batch files to automatically start up screen groups.

You can make batch files with any text editor or word processor. If you use a word processor, make sure that you save the files in ASCII format. You can also make batch files using **COPY CON:** (see Chapter 7).

Batch files can include any OS/2 commands or the names of any programs to run. OS/2 will execute each line in the batch file as it comes to it. Put each command on a new line. If you want to run the batch file in protected mode (the normal OS/2 mode), you must give the file a CMD extension. If you want to run the file in DOS compatibility mode, you must give it a BAT extension. For example, suppose you wanted a command that alphabetically listed all subdirectories of the current directory. You could create a file called DIR-SORT.CMD with the following line:

```
DIR *.* | FIND "<DIR>" | SORT
```

When you type DIRSORT at the OS/2 prompt, OS/2 will make a sorted list of all subdirectories of the current directory.

If there are batch files that you will use only in certain directories, place those batch files in the specific directories. If there are batch files, such as DIRSORT.CMD, that you want to run in any directory, make a special subdirectory, \BATCH, that contains all the batch files. Add \BATCH to the directories listed in your **PATH** command. (See Chapters 7 and 9.)

If you want to stop a batch file, hit Ctrl-C.

Using Command Line Variables in Batch Files

Variables are used to store information. You can assign a value to a variable. Whenever that variable is referenced, it substitutes the value assigned to it. For example, suppose you had a variable called %1 and assigned it the value \LETTERS. If you typed:

```
DIR %1
```

OS/2 would substitute the variable value and thus execute:

```
DIR \LETTERS
```

You can use variables in batch files. Using variables is a very powerful technique because it lets you generalize batch files. Instead of having a batch file for printing a sorted listing of the \BUSINESS directory and having a batch file for printing a sorted listing of the \LETTERS directory, and so forth, you could have one batch file that determines what directory to use by looking at a variable.

You can use up to nine variables in a batch file. Variables are indicated by a % character followed by a number between 1 and 9. You set variable values by typing the values after the batch file name. Variable %n is set to the nth item after the batch file name. For example, suppose you had a batch file called SETUP.CMD. If you typed:

```
SETUP *.* D: hello
```

then %1 would be set to *.*, %2 would be set to D:, and %3 would be set to hello.

You can use the variables within any of the batch file commands. For example, you could change the file DIRSORT to:

```
DIR %1 | FIND "<DIR>" | SORT
```

Then, if you typed:

```
DIRSORT
```

%1 would be set to a blank, and the default directory would be used. If you typed:

```
DIRSORT \ROOSTER
```

%1 would be set to \ROOSTER, and the \ROOSTER directory would be used. If you typed:

```
DIRSORT \OS2*
```

only files in the root directory whose names start with OS2 would be used.

Using Environment Variables in Batch Files

In addition to typing in variables from the command line, you can read in variables set in the environment. This makes it easy to configure a batch file whose variables don't need to change very often. You can read the values of any of the variables set in the environment. Precede and follow the variables with %. For example, suppose you want to concatenate a bunch of files and print them on the printer. Instead of saving the concatenated file in the current directory, you could save it in a directory used for temporary files. You would read the

TEMP value from the environment to determine what drive to use. For example, you could have the following batch file:

```
DIR %1 | FIND "<DIR>" | SORT %TEMP%\TEMP.FIL
DIR %1 | FIND /V "<DIR>" | FIND /V "Volume" | FIND
 /V "Directory" | FIND /V "File(s)" | SORT >>
 %TEMP%\TEMP.FIL
COPY %TEMP%\TEMP.FIL PRN: && ERASE %TEMP%\TEMP.FIL
```

This file makes an alphabetized list of all directories and files in a directory. It uses the value in %1 to determine the directory, sorts the names of all subdirectories, and sticks them in a file called TEMP.FIL on the temporary drive. It then adds a sorted list of all of the files to the end of the temporary file. It prints this file by copying it to the printer. If the file is successfully printed, it is erased.

Note that the commands **PATH, DPATH, PROMPT** set environment values named %PATH%, %DPATH%, and %PROMPT%. The **COMSPEC** option creates a variable called %COMSPEC%. **APPEND** can optionally create a %APPEND% value.

The Batch File Programming Language

In addition to using variables, you can use special programming commands in batch files. These let you set up sections of a batch file to execute if certain things occur, loop through files, and print information on the screen. You can also run other batch files from within a batch file.

An alphabetical listing of the batch programming commands follows. Each entry contains a discussion on the theory and use of the command. As more commands are introduced, the usage examples become more sophisticated. Read about all of the commands before you use the batch file programming language.

CALL	Run another batch file
Function:	This command calls one batch file from within another.
Format:	CALL *name_of_batch_file_to_run* *parameters_for_batch_file*
Comments:	If you run one batch file from within another by simply typing the other batch file's name, the other batch file will run, but when it finishes, control is not returned to the calling program. For example, suppose you have a batch file called SORTALL. You want it to take a list of directory names and run the DIR-SORT batch file on them. If you included the lines:

```
DIRSORT %1
DIRSORT %2
```

within SORTALL, control would transfer to DIRSORT. DIRSORT would be called with the %1 value, but when it finished, no more commands in SORTALL would run. Thus, the line DIRSORT %2 would never be executed.

The **CALL** command gets around this. The other batch file is run, then the calling batch file regains control. For example, if SORTALL contained the lines:

```
CALL DIRSORT %1
CALL DIRSORT %2
```

both commands would be executed.

Use the **CALL** command when you want to run another batch file, and then run some more commands. Don't use the **CALL** command when you want to transfer control to another batch file.

Examples:	You want to create a batch file called SOR-TALL that sorts the directory names and files from three directories, then prints them. You could use:

```
CALL DIRSORT %1
```

```
CALL DIRSORT %2
CALL DIRSORT %3
```

ECHO   Print message

Function: This command sets the **ECHO** mode and can also be used to print messages on the screen.

Format: ECHO [(ON) (OFF) (*text*)]

Comments: When OS/2 executes a batch file, it reads through it line by line. As it interprets each line, it prints the line on the screen. This is called echoing. You can use the **ECHO** command to stop commands from being echoed. You can also use the **ECHO** command to print messages on the screen. By turning off echoing and displaying messages on the screen, you can make your batch files more understandable to users. For example, instead of having the line:

```
DIR %1 | FIND "<DIR>" | SORT >
   %TEMP%\TEMP.FIL
```

appear on the screen, you could print "Sorting directory names."

The **OFF** option prevents commands from being printed on the screen as they are executed.

The **ON** option causes commands to be printed on the screen as they are executed.

If *text* is given, the *text* will be displayed on the screen.

Another way of suppressing echoing is to precede commands with the @ character.

Examples: The following batch file is the same as SORT-ALL, only commands aren't echoed to the screen. Instead, descriptive messages are displayed.

```
@ECHO OFF
ECHO Printing first directory: %1
CALL DIRSORT %1
```

```
ECHO Printing second directory: %2
CALL DIRSORT %2
ECHO Printing third directory: %3
CALL DIRSORT %3
ECHO Finished.
```

ENDLOCAL

and SETLOCAL   Restore and store environment

Function: These commands restore and store the environment. They must be used together.

Format: SETLOCAL
ENDLOCAL

Comments: Normally batch files can modify the environment. For example, if the batch file uses the **CD** command to switch directories, after the batch command finishes, the default directory will still be switched. Most times, you want this to occur. However, a batch file might want to modify the environment and then restore the original environment. This is useful if the batch file needs to guarantee certain **PATH** or **DPATH** settings, change directories, or modify the environment in some other way.

If your batch file contains environment-altering commands that you only want to affect the environment temporarily, put them between a **STARTLOCAL** and **ENDLOCAL** pair.

Examples: Suppose your batch file does a lot of work in the TEMP drive. You could:

```
SETLOCAL
CD \OS2SYS
%TEMP%
COPY C:*.*
ENDLOCAL
```

After the batch file runs, the original drive and directory will be unchanged.

EXTPROC   Specify batch processor

Function: This command selects an alternative batch processor.

Format: EXTPROC   *batch_processor_name*   [*batch_proc_parameters*]

Comments: Normally OS/2 processes batch files. This command specifies a program to process the batch files instead of OS/2. Advanced users can use this feature to create their own batch file language. If this command is used, it must be the first line in the batch file.

Examples: Suppose you have created a program called REXX.EXE that processes the REXX batch file language. You have stored this file in the \ALTPROG directory of the C drive. You could tell OS/2 to use REXX.EXE as the batch file interpreter by using the following as the first line in a batch file:

```
EXTPROC C:\ALTPROG\REXX.EXE
```

FOR   Repeat on a set

Function: This command causes a set of actions to occur for all elements in a set.

Format: FOR %%*letter* IN (*item_list*) DO *command*

Comments: If you want to repeat a command for a set of files but the command doesn't accept wild cards, you can use the **FOR** command. It is also useful when you want to perform a series of sequential operations on an item.

    Letter can be any single letter, such as A. For example, %%*letter*, or %%A, is a variable. It gets sequentially set to the items in *item_list*. Suppose *item_list* is: \LETTERS \BUSINESS \CLASSES. %%A will get set to \LETTERS, and *command* will be executed. Then %%A will be set to \BUSINESS and *command* will be executed. Finally, %%A will be set to \CLASSES and *command* will be executed. *Command* is any OS/2 command or program file. It can use the value of %%A. *Item_list* can contain wild cards. For example, if you set *item_list* to *.TXT, %%A would be set to all of the files in the default directory that had an extension of TXT.

Examples:

Suppose you want to type all batch files in the current directory and copy them to the D drive. You could:

```
FOR %%A IN ( *.CMD ) DO TYPE %%A & COPY
    %%A D:
```

GOTO

Go to a label

Function:

This command lets you jump to a different part of a batch file.

Format:

GOTO *label*

Comments:

Normally OS/2 processes batch commands one after the other. Sometimes, however, you want to execute one set of commands if one condition holds true and another set of commands if the condition doesn't hold true.

There are two ways to use the **GOTO** command. The first is with the **&&** or **||** commands. These let you jump to a set of batch file routines if a certain DOS command worked (**&&**) or didn't work (**||**). You can also use the **GOTO** command with the **IF** command, covered next.

You indicate the part of the batch file to jump to by setting *label*. *Label* gets set to the name of any section label in the batch file. A section label is a word or words, preceded by a colon, that you can place anywhere in the batch file. The label name can include spaces and numbers, but not punctuation marks.

For example, you could have the following:

```
:LOOP
ECHO This is an endless loop.
GOTO LOOP
```

See also: IF

Examples: The following batch file creates a file that tracks how long a user has been working at the computer. The user types **LOG** at the start of a session and then **LOG** at the end. When the user types **LOG** the second time, the program will print the current time and the time that the user started.

Before you run this batch file, you must create a text file that contains a carriage return. To do this, type:

```
COPY CON: CR
```

Then hit Enter and Ctrl-Z.

Here is the listing of the batch file:

```
ECHO OFF
DIR LOG.FIL && GOTO LOGOUT
ECHO Welcome to the computer system.
DATE < CR > LOG.FIL
TIME < CR >> LOG.FIL
GOTO LOGEND
:LOGOUT
ECHO I hope you had a good work day.
ECHO You started at:
TYPE LOG.FIL
ECHO It is now:
DATE < CR
TIME < CR
DEL LOG.FIL
:LOGEND
ECHO ON
```

IF   Check condition

Function: This command determines if a condition is met.

Format:

IF [NOT] ERRORLEVEL *number command*
IF [NOT] *string1* == *string2 command*
IF [NOT] EXIST *filename command*

Comments:

The **IF** command lets you execute a command only if a certain condition is true.

You can use the **ERRORLEVEL** feature to execute a command depending upon the error code returned by a program or OS/2 command. In general, the error code is greater than 0 if an error occurred. The command indicated will be executed if the error code is greater than or equal to *number*.

For example, the following will jump to an error section if the **COPY** command didn't work:

```
COPY ROBDIG.LET D:
IF ERRORLEVEL 1 GOTO ERROR
GOTO FINISHED
:ERROR
ECHO Sorry, the file ROBDIG.LET doesn't
 exist.
:FINISHED
```

The **NOT** option causes the command to be executed if the condition doesn't hold true.

You can use the *string1* == *string2* format to execute a command if a string has a particular value. Usually, one of the strings is set to a variable, such as %1 or %%A. This lets you execute different commands depending upon the setting of a variable.

If you want to check a value that may be empty or contain spaces, you should first enclose the value in double quotes. In other words, you could:

```
IF "%1" == "" GOTO END
```

to check to see if parameter 1 is empty. Or you could:

```
IF "%YALEHARV%" == "Big Three" GOTO END
```

The **EXIST** format executes the command if the file exists.

See also: **GOTO**

Examples: Suppose you want to make a batch file that helps employees format floppy disks. You want to make sure that they don't accidentally format your hard disk. First, you rename the **FORMAT** command to FRM.COM, so that no one accidentally uses it. (The **FORMAT** command is stored as FORMAT.COM in the \OS2 directory.) Then you create the following batch file, called FORMAT.CMD. Its format is:

```
FORMAT drive option1 option2
```

where the options are the parameters that can be given to the **FORMAT** command.

```
ECHO OFF
ECHO Floppy disk formatter
IF "%1" == "A:" GOTO FORMAT FLOPPY
IF "%1" == "B:" GOTO FORMAT FLOPPY
ECHO I'm sorry, but you can't format
 that drive
GOTO END
:FORMAT FLOPPY
FRM %1 %2 %3
:END
```

PAUSE Wait for key press

Function: This command stops a batch file until the user presses a key.

Format: PAUSE

Comments: Sometimes you may want to give the user a chance to perform an action before a batch file continues. For example, you may want to give the user a chance to insert a particular disk in a drive. Using the **PAUSE** command also gives the user a chance to hit Ctrl-C before a critical action occurs.

You may want to use the **ECHO** command to display some text before you use the **PAUSE** command. The pause command will display "Strike a key when ready . . ." and wait for the user to hit a key.

Examples: The following program copies the LOG.FIL file to a floppy disk. It prints a message if the file already exists and gives the user a chance to stop the copying.

```
ECHO OFF
ECHO This command copies the time log
  information to
ECHO a floppy in the A drive.
ECHO Please insert a floppy in the A
  drive.
PAUSE
IF NOT EXIST A:LOG.FIL GOTO COPYIT
ECHO There is already a log file on the
ECHO disk. If you want to write over
  this information,
ECHO hit Return. If not, hold down the
  Ctrl key and
ECHO hit the letter C.
PAUSE
:COPYIT
COPY LOG.FIL A:
```

REM   Remark
Function: This command lets you put comments inside a batch file.

Format: REM *text*
Comments: Sometimes you may wish to annotate a batch file so that you know what all of the lines do. You can use the **REM** command to add comments. These comments are not printed on the screen; they are for you to read if you edit the batch file.

Examples: The following program has comments:

```
@ECHO OFF
REM File: DIRDIR.CMD
REM Format: DIRDIR directory_name
REM
REM This batch file sorts the names of
 all files in
REM a directory.
REM
REM See if the directory exists.
IF NOT EXIST %1 GOTO ERROR
REM Sort the names of all the files.
 Use the
REM /V option of FIND to exclude
 directories REM and the heading.
DIR %1 | FIND /V "<DIR>" | FIND /V
"Volume" | FIND /V "Directory" | FIND
/V "File(s)" | SORT
REM Now leave.
GOTO END
:ERROR
REM Print an error message.
ECHO Sorry, that directory doesn't
 exist.
:END
REM quit
```

If you don't pass any parameters to this batch file, %1 will not have a value. This will cause the IF NOT EXIST %1 GOTO ERROR line to print an error message, but the program will run correctly.

SHIFT   Shift command line parameters

Function: This command shifts command line parameter values.

Format: SHIFT

Comments: Normally batch files can use up to nine parameters, all entered on the command line.

The **SHIFT** command lets you access more than nine parameters. When the **SHIFT** command is executed, the variable %n gets the value previously in the variable %n + 1. For example, after a shift command, %2 gets what used to be in %3, and %9 gets what would be the tenth command line parameter.

You can use this command to access more than nine command line parameters or to execute a set of commands for each of a variable number of command line parameters.

Examples: Suppose you want to make a batch file called SORTALL2 that calls the DIRSORT batch file for any number of directories. You could:

```
@ECHO OFF
REM This file creates a sorted listing
 of any number
REM of directories. It repeatedly calls
 DIRSORT.
REM Its format is:
REM SORTALL2 [directory name] [...]
REM
REM Sort the first directory. Note that
 this is done
REM before shifting so that the default
 directory will
REM be used if no parameters were
 entered.
REM
:SORTIT
CALL DIRSORT %1
REM Now shift over the values.
SHIFT
REM See if there are any more
 directories to use.
IF "%1" == "" GOTO END
GOTO SORTIT
REM Now we are finished.
```

```
:END
```

Note that you must create the DIRSORT.CMD
batch file before you run this program.

Summary

- Batch files are an easy way of grouping OS/2 commands to create powerful new commands.
- Batch files are text files that have a .CMD or .BAT extension.
- Batch files contain a list of OS/2 commands or program names to execute.
- You can pass parameters to the batch file by typing values on the command line.
- You can pass parameters to the batch file through the environment.
- There is a batch file programming language that lets you make very sophisticated batch files.

10

Configuring the System

In this chapter you'll learn how to automatically configure your system, using the STARTUP.CMD, OS2INIT.CMD, AUTOEXEC.BAT, and CONFIG.SYS files.

The System Initialization Files

There are four files that characterize the OS/2 system: CONFIG.SYS, STARTUP.CMD, OS2INIT.CMD, and AUTOEXEC.BAT. When OS2 starts up, it reads the CONFIG.SYS file to determine what device drivers to load, what country format to use, and what parameters to use for the multitasker.

OS/2 then executes the STARTUP.CMD batch file. The primary use of this batch file is to automatically start screen groups. If this batch file doesn't exist, the Session Manager starts.

When an OS/2 screen group starts, it begins by executing OS2INIT.CMD. This batch file is used to set up **PATH** and **DPATH** values, and to manipulate the prompt or execute customizing utilities.

When the DOS compatibility mode screen group starts, AUTOEXEC.BAT runs. This functions similarly to OS2INIT.CMD. It sets up the **PATH** and **APPEND** command and any customization necessary. It is essentially the same as the AUTOEXEC.BAT in DOS systems.

The STARTUP.CMD File

When you first turn on your computer, OS/2 runs several system programs to initialize the computer. It then runs a batch file called STARTUP.CMD. You can edit this batch file to specially configure your system.

The STARTUP.CMD batch file can contain any of the batch file commands. It is like any other batch file, only it automatically runs when OS/2 is started. Use the STARTUP.CMD file to automatically start screen groups. For example, you can use it to start your word processor and spreadsheet.

If you want to return to the Session Manager after starting programs, place the **EXIT** command at the end of the STARTUP.CMD file.

For example, the following STARTUP.CMD will start a word processor called WP and an analysis package called DESTINATION. It will then start up the Session Manager:

```
REM This is a sample STARTUP.CMD file.
START "Word Processor" C:\WP\WP
START "Analysis" C:\DEST\DEST
REM Now return to the Session Manager.
EXIT
```

The OS2INIT.CMD File

Each time you start a new OS2 screen group, the OS2INIT.CMD file runs. This lets you set up **PATH** statements and otherwise modify the environment.[1]

Your OS2INIT.CMD should contain a **PATH** statement so that OS/2 can automatically find program files. Be sure to include the root directory of the boot drive and the OS2 directory in this list. Set up **DPATH** directories in a like fashion as well. Include the root directory of the boot drive, OS2, and any directories containing information files for the **HELP** or **HELPMSG** commands.

If your system doesn't have a hardware clock, add **DATE** and **TIME** statements. If you want to modify the **PROMPT**, do it next. Then run any programs that you want to run before using the system. For example, you might want to run programs that change the screen color.

Thus, an outline of a STARTUP.CMD file is:

```
PATH statement
DPATH statement
DATE statement
TIME statement
PROMPT statement
Initialization programs
```

The AUTOEXEC.BAT File

The first time you open the DOS compatibility mode screen group, OS/2 runs a batch file called AUTOEXEC.BAT. It ser-

[1] Some prerelease versions of OS/2 do not run the OS2INIT.CMD batch file when new OS/2 sessions start. If your version doesn't, create a Session Manager option for the Start a Program with *Start an OS/2 Session* as the program title and OS2INIT.CMD as the program name. Look at the program names for the other programs in the Start a Program list. Replace them with your own batch files that first **CALL** OS2INIT.CMD; then execute the program listed in the Start a Program list. A quicker way is to add /K OS2INIT.CMD to the PROTSHELL line in CONFIG.SYS.

ves the same purpose as STARTUP.CMD, only it runs in DOS compatibility mode. You can use any DOS compatibility mode commands in AUTOEXEC.BAT. It should have a similar format to the STARTUP.CMD file:

```
PATH statement
APPEND statement
PROMPT statement
Initialization programs
Application to start
```

The CONFIG.SYS File

The CONFIG.SYS file is an extremely important file. It describes many important aspects of the system to OS/2. For example, it tells the number of disk buffers to use, the temporary drives to use for virtual memory swapping, whether the DOS compatibility mode is appropriate, and what country settings to use. It also loads drivers for peripherals and sets up memory-resident programs that all screen groups can see, such as the print spooler.

In general, the default settings in the CONFIG.SYS file are appropriate, and only advanced users should modify them. Most applications that require modifications to the CONFIG.SYS file should make the changes themselves.

The CONFIG.SYS file is a normal ASCII file that contains any number of configuration commands. Each of these commands is discussed in the alphabetical listing in this chapter. Be sure to read over the list of commands carefully before you make any changes to the CONFIG.SYS file.

Users outside of the United States might need to use **CODEPAGE, COUNTRY**, and **DEVINFO**. Intermediate users might use **BREAK, BUFFERS, DEVICE, DISKCACHE, LIBPATH, PROTECTONLY, REM, RMSIZE, RUN** and **SWAPPATH**. Advanced users might use **IOPL, MAXWAIT, MEMMAN, PRIORITY, PROTSHELL, SHELL, THREADS**, and **TIMESLICE**.

The **DEVICE, DEVINFO, REM**, and **RUN** statements can be used several times in the CONFIG.SYS file. All other commands can only be used once.

Any changes you make to the CONFIG.SYS file take effect the next time you reboot or start up the system.

BREAK	Set Ctrl-C check
Function:	This command sets Ctrl-C checking for DOS compatibility mode.
Format:	BREAK = (ON) (OFF)
Default:	BREAK = OFF
Comments:	This command applies to the DOS compatibility mode only. Except for its format, it is exactly the same as the OS/2 **BREAK** command.
Examples:	To automatically set Ctrl-C checking on in DOS compatibility mode, you could insert the following line in your CONFIG.SYS file: BREAK = ON

BUFFERS	Set number of buffers
Function:	This command sets the number of disk buffers that OS/2 uses.
Format:	BUFFERS = *number_of_buffers*
Default:	BUFFERS = 3
Comments:	When OS/2 reads from the disk, it temporarily stores the information in a disk buffer. The next time it accesses the information, it can read from the buffer instead of from the disk. This speeds up disk access.
	Each disk buffer is 512 bytes, the size of a typical sector. You can set between 1 and 99 disk buffers. Using 10 to 20 buffers should be fine for most applications. If you have a lot of subdirectories, you might want to use as many as 30 buffers.

Examples: You want OS/2 to use 25 disk buffers. You
                 would include the following line:
                 BUFFERS = 25

CODEPAGE   Select code page
Function: This command lets you override the default
                 code page selection.
Format: CODEPAGE = *primary_code_page* [, *secon-
                 dary_code_page*]
Default: Chosen from monitor, keyboard, printer, and
                 COUNTRY statement.
Comments: The code page determines how OS/2 will dis-
                 play characters. It is used for displaying the
                 alphabets from different countries. The
                 COUNTRY command makes a default selec-
                 tion of code pages. You can use the
                 CODEPAGE command to override the selec-
                 tion **COUNTRY** makes.
                 As the format indicates, the system can only
                 have two available code pages. Select these
                 values from the following table:

Code Page
Number	Country
437	United States
850	Multilingual
860	Portuguese
863	Canadian-French
865	Nordic

                 You must also include a **DEVINFO** com-
                 mand for all devices on which you will switch
                 code pages.
See also: **COUNTRY, DEVINFO, CHCP** in Chapter 6
Examples: Suppose you want the two available code
                 pages to be Portuguese and Canadian-
                 French. You would use:
                 CODEPAGE = 860, 863

COUNTRY   Select country

Function: This command configures the keyboard and display for various countries.

Format: COUNTRY = *country_number*

Default: COUNTRY = 001

Comments: Different countries use different alphabet symbols and keyboard layouts. The **COUNTRY** command selects the keyboard layout and character set (code page) appropriate for various countries. It also selects time, date, currency, and case conventions.

Select *country_number* from the following table. An asterisk next to the name means that support for the code page may not have been developed yet:

Country	Number	Code Page	Keyboard Code (Keybxx)
*Arab	785	437	
*Asia (English)	099	437,850	
Australia	061	437,850	
Belgium	032	437,850	BE
Canada (English)	001	437,850	
Canada (French)	002	863,850	CF
*China (PRC)	086		
Denmark	045	865,850	DK
Finland	358	437,850	SU
France	033	437,850	FR
Germany	049	437,850	GR
*Israel	972	437	
Italy	039	437,850	IT
*Japan	081		
*Korea	082		
Latin America	003	437,850	LA
Netherlands	031	437,850	NL

Norway	047	865,850	NO
Portugal	351	860,850	PO
Spain	034	437,850	SP
Sweden	046	437,850	SV
Switzerland	041	437,850	SF,SG
*Taiwan	088		
United Kingdom	044	437,850	UK
United States	001	437,850	US

Examples: If you are using your computer in the United Kingdom, you could:
COUNTRY = 044

DEVICE   Install device driver

Function: This command installs an OS/2 device driver.

Format: DEVICE = [*drive_name:*] [*path*] *device_driver* [*arguments*]

Default: None

Comments: Many hardware boards need device drivers to let them communicate with the computer. These boards come with device driver software and software to install the driver. This installation software will automatically modify CONFIG.SYS. If the board doesn't come with such installation software, you will have to use the **DEVICE** command yourself.

There are also device drivers that let you create RAM disks and take further advantage of hardware that does not normally need a device driver. These are detailed at the end of this chapter.

Place a **DEVICE** statement in CONFIG.SYS for each driver that you want to install.

The following device drivers come with OS/2:

ANSI.SYS— Supports the ANSI control characters in DOS compatibility mode

COM0x.SYS— Supports asynchronous communications for serial ports

EGA.SYS—Supports mouse use with EGA modes 14, 15, and 16

EXTDSKDD.SYS—Supports external floppy disk drives

MOUSE*xxx*.SYS—Supports different mice; *xxx* selects the mouse

POINTDD.SYS—Supports mouse pointer

VDISK.SYS—Creates a RAM disk

This command is primarily for use by advanced users. The parameters for the device drivers that come with OS/2 are documented at the end of this chapter.

Note: You do not need to use the **DEVICE** command in order for your system to operate. In fact, standard hardware (such as parallel printers, the internal hard disk and floppy drive, the display screen, and keyboard) will work well even if you don't have a CONFIG.SYS file. However, add-on hardware such as external floppy drives, cartridge disk systems, and custom monitors require a **DEVICE** statement if you plan to use them.

Examples: Suppose you want to create a 32K RAM disk. You could:

`DEVICE = C:\OS2SYS\VDISK.SYS 32`

DEVINFO Prepares devices for code page switching

Function: This command prepares devices for code page switching.

Format: DEVINFO = *device_type*, *sub_type*, [*drive*] [*path*] *table_file_name* [ROM = (*code_page1* [, *code_page1*])]

Default: None

Comments: In order to support code pages on the various hardware devices, you must use **DEVINFO** to give OS/2 information about each device.

Set *device_type* to one of the following: KBD, PRN, LPT1, LPT2, LPT3, or SCR. Use KBD for the keyboard, PRN, LPT1, LPT2, and LPT3 for printers, and SCR for the screen.

Set *sub_type* to the physical device type. This indicates a particular type of device. For the keyboard, use the two-letter keyboard code. For the screen use EGA, VGA, or BGA. Use 4201 for the IBM Proprinter and 5202 for the IBM Quietwriter printers.

Set *table_file_name* to the name of the file that contains the code page tables for the device. Use KEYBOARD.DCP for the keyboard. Use VIOTBL.DCP for the screen. Use the printer sub_type.DCP for the printer. These files will be in the root directory or the OS2SYS directory.

The ROM option lets you list one or two code pages available in device ROM or on a device cartridge. The code pages must be those specified with the **CODEPAGE** statement. This can only be used with a printer.

Examples: You want to set up your screen and keyboard for code page switching. You have an EGA board and you plan to use the US keyboard. You would use:

```
COUNTRY = 001
CODEPAGE = 437,850
DEVINFO = KBD,US,C:\KEYBOARD.DCP
DEVINFO = SCR,EGA,C:\VIOTBL.DCP
```

DISKCACHE   Set disk cache size
   IBM OS/2 Only

Function: This command sets the size of the OS/2 disk cache.

Format: DISKCACHE = *cache_size*

Default: 64

Comments: This command is available only for IBM PS/2 Models 50, 60, and 80. It sets the size of the disk cache buffer. Set *cache_size* to the size of the buffer in kilobytes. It must be a number between 64 and 7200.

Choosing a higher number results in faster disk access but less free RAM.

Examples: You are doing a great deal of disk-intensive work. Therefore you decide to increase the size of the disk cache. You could use:

`DISKCACHE = 160`

FCBS

Function:

Format:

Default:

Comments:

Selects the number of file control blocks

This command selects the number of file control blocks. It is for DOS compatibility mode only.

FCBS = *number_of_files, number_to_not_close*

FCBS = 4,0

This command is for DOS compatibility mode only. It selects the number of file control blocks that OS/2 can have open at one time. If a program tries to open more files than specified, OS/2 will shut down files to make room. OS/2 will not shut down the first *number_to_not_close* files when doing so.

Most DOS programs will not need this command. Only include it if you have applications that specifically require it.

IOPL

Function:

Format:

Default:

Comments:

Select I/O privilege level

This command selects the I/O privilege level.

IOPL = (YES) (NO)

IOPL = NO

Normally, OS/2 does not allow programs to directly access the hardware. This is to prevent conflicts during multitasking. Some programs, however, need to do low-level interaction with the hardware. To run such programs, you must set IOPL to YES.

Applications which need the IOPL set to YES will specifically indicate so. If you don't run such programs, keep IOPL to NO.

Examples: You need to allow a certain program to directly access hardware:

```
IOPL = YES
```

LIBPATH   Set DDL directory

Function: This command specifies the directory in which dynamic link library modules will be located.

Format: LIBPATH = *drive:path* [;*drive2:path*] [...]

Default: Root directory of the system disk

Comments: OS/2 programs can load functions that they need dynamically. This means that they do not have to include code for all of the system calls that they make; thus, the programs take less room. The **LIBPATH** specifies where the dynamic link libraries will be located. The directories specified will be searched in the order they are listed.

Examples: You want to put dynamic link libraries in the \OS2SYS directory and in a \MYLIB directory. You would:

```
LIBPATH = C:\OS2SYS;C:\MYLIB
```

MAXWAIT   Set process wait time

Function: This command sets the maximum time a process will wait before it gets an increase in priority.

Format: MAXWAIT = *wait_time*

Default: MAXWAIT = 3

Comments: OS/2 rapidly flips between concurrent programs. This command sets the maximum amount of time a process can go without processor time. After this amount of time, the process gets a priority boost. The time is given in seconds.

Examples:	Suppose you want any processes that haven't gotten processor time after 4 seconds to be given time. You would: `MAXWAIT = 4`

MEMMAN	Set memory management options
Function:	This command sets whether memory can be swapped and moved.
Format:	MEMMAN = SWAP, MOVE MEMMAN = NOSWAP, MOVE MEMMAN = NOSWAP, NOMOVE
Default:	If booted from a hard disk: MEMMAN = SWAP, MOVE If booted from a floppy: MEMMAN = NOSWAP, MOVE
Comments:	When programs need more memory than the system currently has available, OS/2 can temporarily copy sections of RAM to disk and then use the RAM for the process that needs it. This is called *swapping*. It lets several processes run at the same time, even if there is not enough RAM for the data each of them uses. The **SWAP** option allows swapping to occur. The **NOSWAP** option prevents it. When many programs are running, OS/2 can more efficiently allocate memory if it can relocate the actual areas to which the memory addresses refer. **MOVE** allows OS/2 to do this; **NOMOVE** prevents it. MEMMAN = NOSWAP, NOMOVE should only be used for dedicated systems.
Examples:	You want to optimize the memory that your applications can use. You are on a hard disk system; therefore, disk access is fast and there is a lot of disk space. You use: `MEMMAN = SWAP, MOVE`

PRIORITY Set priority selection

Function: This command tells OS/2 how to determine the priority of concurrent processes.

Format: PRIORITY = (ABSOLUTE) (DYNAMIC)

Default: PRIORITY = DYNAMIC

Comments: When several programs (or processes) are running at the same time, OS/2 quickly switches between each of the programs, giving each a little piece of CPU time. OS/2 uses a scheduling algorithm to determine which program to give CPU time to at any given moment. Some processes are determined *time critical* — these are given highest priority. Some are called *normal*, and some are called *idle*. Each of these classifications has 32 priority levels as well.

Normally OS/2 determines priority based upon what a routine is doing and its previous priority levels. This is what occurs with dynamic priority allocation. The **ABSOLUTE** option instructs OS/2 to assign priority on a first come, first served basis.

Most users will not need to use this option.

PROTECTONLY Select DOS compatibility mode option

Function: This command sets whether or not the DOS compatibility mode will be supported.

Format: PROTECTONLY = (YES) (NO)

Default: PROTECTONLY = NO

Comments: Normally OS/2 lets you run protected mode programs — the normal, multitasking OS/2 programs — and DOS compatibility mode programs. But, OS/2 sets aside a lot of memory in order to provide the DOS compatibility mode option. (Typically, 640K is set aside.) If you know that you won't be using programs designed just for DOS, you can increase the amount of memory you have available by setting **PROTECTONLY** to **YES**.

Examples: Because you will only run programs specifically designed for OS/2, you decide to save memory resources by removing the DOS compatibility mode option:
```
PROTECTONLY = YES
```

PROTSHELL   Selects alternate Session Manager

Function: This command selects a Session Manager (user interface shell) other than the normal one.

Format: PROTSHELL = [*drive_name*:] [*path_name*] *shell_program* [*shell_program_arguments*]

Default: OS/2 Session Manager, which is:

PROTSHELL = DMPC.EXE SHELL11F.CNF
   SHELL11F.EXE CMD.EXE

or

PROTSHELL = DMPC.EXE SHELL11F.CNF
   SHELL11F.EXE CMD.EXE /K
   OS2INIT.CMD

Comments: This command is for advanced users only. You can use it to specify a user interface shell other than the Session Manager. You can also use it to specify a command processor other than CMD.EXE.

   If you change the command processor, be sure to also change **COMSPEC**.

RMSIZE   Sets memory to reserve for DOS compatibility mode

Function: This command determines the amount of memory that OS/2 will set aside for its DOS compatibility mode.

Format: RMSIZE = *kilobytes_to_reserve*

Default: If extended memory is installed, RMSIZE = 640K or RMSIZE = 512K. If no extended memory is installed, RMSIZE is the total amount of memory minus the minimum amount needed for protected mode.

Comments: As mentioned in the discussion of PROTEC-TONLY, OS/2 reserves memory for use by the DOS compatibility mode. Protected mode programs cannot access this memory. The RMSIZE command lets you select the amount of memory reserved for DOS compatibility mode. If you plan to use programs in the DOS compatibility mode but know that they don't need 640K, you can use this option to give protected mode programs more RAM to use. Because OS/2 uses virtual memory, having more RAM speeds programs.

Examples: You need to run some programs in the DOS compatibility mode. From reading the documentation on these programs, you determine that they need 384K memory at most. Therefore, you use the RMSIZE option so that protected mode programs have more RAM to use:

```
RMSIZE = 384
```

RUN Autostart programs

Function: This command lets you start detachable and monitor programs during system initialization.

Format: RUN = [*drive:*] [*path*] *program_name*
[*program_parameters*]

Default: None

Comments: This command lets you automatically start detachable and monitor programs during system initialization. You can have more than one **RUN** statement in CONFIG.SYS. The applications that start must be specially designed to run without user input or output or to receive user input through a pop-up window. Programs started by **RUN** are similar to DOS memory-resident utilities.

Use the **RUN** statement for programs that intercept the keyboard values to bring up a pop-up display or for detachable programs, such as the print spooler, that need to be accessible by all screen groups.

See also: **START**

Examples: You want to start the print spooler automatically. You could include the following line:

```
RUN C:\OS2\SPOOL.EXE
```

REM   Comment

Function: This command lets you imbed comments in a CONFIG.SYS file.

Format: REM [*comment*]

Default: none

Comments: This command lets you place comments within a CONFIG.SYS file. You can use it to explain why you made certain selections so that you will be able to understand the CONFIG.SYS file better if you or someone else needs to modify it.

Examples: You might include the following comments:

```
REM ** The following line selects the
  display device.
REM ** Change EGA to VGA if you add a
  VGA board.
REM ** Make sure that the VIOTBL.DCP
  file is in the
REM ** root directory. If it is not,
  change the
REM ** path name appropriately.
REM
DEVINFO = SCR, EGA, C:\VIOTBL.DCP
```

SHELL   Select DOS compatibility mode command
                   processor

Function: This command selects the program to use to
                   process commands in the DOS compatibility
                   mode.

Format: SHELL = [*drive*:] [*path*] *program_name*
                   [*parameters*]

Default: SHELL = COMMAND.COM /P

Comments: In general, this command is used to enlarge
                   the environment of DOS compatibility mode.
                   To do so, use COMMAND.COM as the shell,
                   and set the **/P** and **/E** options.

                   Advanced users can use this command to
                   specify an alternative command line proces-
                   sor.

Examples: You want to allow a 1K environment for DOS
                   compatibility mode programs. You could:

                   SHELL = C:\OS2SYS\COMMAND.COM /E:1024 /P

SWAPPATH   Set swap file location

Function: This command sets the directory OS/2 will
                   use for memory swapping.

Format: SWAPPATH = *drive*: [*directory*]

Default: SWAPPATH = C:\

Comments: When OS/2 swaps memory (see **MEMMAN**),
                   it does so by temporarily copying sections of
                   memory to a disk file. The **SWAPPATH** com-
                   mand lets you specify what drive and direc-
                   tory to use for this swap file. Memory
                   swapping will be quicker if you use your
                   quickest drive as the swap drive.

Examples: You have two disk drives: the C drive, which
                   is a cartridge hard disk that you use for boot-
                   ing, and the D drive, which is a high-speed
                   hard disk. So that memory swapping will be
                   as fast as possible, you include:

                   SWAPPATH = D:\

THREADS   Set maximum number of threads

Function: This command sets the maximum number of threads that can run in OS/2.

Format: THREADS = *number_of_threads*

Default: THREADS = 48

Comments: OS/2 programs can define a bunch of processes to run concurrently. Each concurrent process is called a *thread*. The **THREADS** command sets the maximum number of threads that can run at once. This limits the number of programs that can run at once. Note, however, that this doesn't set the number of programs that can run at once, because single programs can have multiple threads. Increasing the maximum number of threads decreases system RAM.

Number_of_threads can be between 16 and 255.

Examples: You need to run many multithread applications. Thus, you decide to raise the threads limit to 80:

```
THREADS = 80
```

TIMESLICE   Set time slice values

Function: This command determines the minimum and maximum amounts of time to use for each time slice.

Format: TIMESLICE = *min_time* [, *max_time*]

Default: Set by OS/2

Comments: When OS/2 runs concurrent processes, it quickly flips among them, giving each a bit of CPU time. **TIMESLICE** sets the minimum and maximum amount of CPU time that OS/2 will give any application during one time slice. This also controls how quickly OS/2 switches among applications.

Both times are in milliseconds. *Min_time* must be greater than 31; *max_time* must be at least *min_time*.

Do not use this command unless an application specifically requests you to do so.

The Installable Device Drivers

Installable device drivers let you take advantage of special aspects of peripherals. They also allow OS/2 to use nonstandard peripherals. All device drivers are added with the **DEVICE** command in the CONFIG.SYS file.

The device drivers that come with OS/2 are discussed in the following pages. Peripherals may also come with their own device drivers and should include instructions on using them.

ANSI.SYS	Real mode ANSI support
Format:	ANSI.SYS
Comments:	This driver supports ANSI escape sequences in the DOS compatibility mode.
Examples:	You want to support ANSI sequences in DOS compatibility mode. The file ANSI.SYS is in the \OS2SYS directory. You would add: `DEVICE = \OS2SYS\ANSI.SYS`

COM.SYS	Asynchronous communication support
Format:	COM01.SYS COM02.SYS
Comments:	This driver lets OS/2 programs, such as the print spooler, use serial ports. Use COM02.SYS for IBM PS/2 computers and COM01.SYS for IBM ATs, XT 286s, and compatibles. COM01.SYS supports COM1 and COM2. COM02.SYS supports COM1, COM2, and COM3.

See also: SETCOM40

Examples: You want to use COM1 with your IBM PS/2
                    80. You would include:
                    DEVICE = C:\OS2SYS\COM02.SYS

EGA.SYS   Extended EGA service

Format: EGA.SYS

Comments: This driver lets you use the mouse with EGA
                    modes 14, 15, and 16. Software documenta-
                    tion will indicate if this driver should be
                    loaded.

Examples: A software package indicates it needs the
                    EGA.SYS driver. You could add:
                    DEVICE = C:\OS2SYS\EGA.SYS

EXTDSKDD.SYS External floppy support

Format: EXTDSKDD.SYS /D:*drive_number* [/C]
                    [/F:*device_type*] [/H:*max_head*] [/N]
                    [/S:*sectors_per_track*] [/T:*tracks_per_
                    side*]

Comments: This driver lets OS/2 use external floppy disk
                    drives.

                    Use **/D** to select the drive number. The first
                    external drive number is drive 2. This num-
                    ber can be between 0 and 255.

                    Use **/C** to indicate that the drive can deter-
                    mine if the drive door is closed or not.

                    Use **/F** to indicate that type of drive where:
                        0 = SS or DS/DD (360K) 5 1/4-inch drive
                        1 = high-density (1.2M) 5 1/4-inch drive
                        2 = low-density (720K) 3 1/2-inch drive
                    The default is 2.

                    Use **/H** to indicate the maximum head num-
                    ber. The default is 2. This number can be be-
                    tween 1 and 99.

                    Use **/N** to indicate a hard or otherwise non-
                    removable disk.

Use **/S** to indicate the number of sectors per track. This can be from 1 to 99. The default is 9.

Use **/T** to indicate the number of tracks per side. This can range from 1 to 999. The default is 80.

Examples: You want to add an external 5 1/4-inch drive to your PS/2. You would add:

```
DEVICE = C:\OS2SYS\EXTDSKDD.SYS /D:02
/F:0 /T:40
```

MOUSExxx.SYS Mouse support

Format: MOUSE*XXX*.SYS [,serial = *port*] [,mode = *proc_modes*] [,qsize = *buffer_size*]

Comments: This driver lets OS/2 use mice.

Set *xxx* to select the type of mouse. Use the following for IBM ATs and XT 286s:

A00 PC Mouse by Mouse Systems

A01   Visi-On Mouse

A02   Microsoft Bus Mouse (serial)

A03   Microsoft Bus Mouse (parallel)

A05   Microsoft InPort Mouse

Use the following for IBM PS/2s:

B00   PC Mouse by Mouse Systems

B01   Visi-On Mouse

B02   Microsoft Bus Mouse (serial)

B05   IBM In-board Mouse

Set *port* to COM1 or COM2 if it is a serial mouse on an IBM AT or XT 286. On an IBM PS/2, *port* can be COM1 through COM8. The default for a serial mouse is COM1.

Use *proc_modes* to set if the mouse will be supported in real mode, protected mode, or both. Use **R** for real mode only, **P** for protected mode only, and **B** for both.

Set *buffer_size* to the size of the buffer for mouse movements. The number can be between 1 and 100. The default is 10.

Examples: You plan to use a Microsoft parallel mouse for
                 your computer. You could:
                 DEVICE = C:\OS2SYS\MOUSEA03.SYS

POINTDD.SYS Mouse pointer support
Format: POINTDD.SYS
Comments: This driver lets a mouse pointer be drawn.
See also: MOUSE*xxx*.SYS, EGA.SYS
Examples: You want a pointer to track the mouse move-
                 ment. Include:
                 DEVICE = C:\OS2SYS\POINTDD.SYS

VDISK.SYS   Creates RAM disk
Format: VDISK.SYS [*disk_size*] [,*sector_size*]
                 [,*root_entries*]
Comments: This driver creates a RAM disk. A RAM disk is
                 much faster than any other disk; however, it
                 uses memory that could otherwise be used by
                 programs.
                 Set *disk_size* to the size of the RAM disk in
                 kilobytes. The default is 64; the minimum is
                 16.
                 Set *sector_size* to the size of the sectors, in
                 bytes. The default is 128. The values can be
                 128, 256, 512, or 1024.
                 Set *root_entries* to the maximum number of
                 root directory entries. The default is 64.
                 Values can range from 2 to 1024.
Examples: You want to create an 800K RAM disk. You
                 would:
                 DEVICE = RAMDISK 800

Summary

- The STARTUP.CMD file runs when OS/2 is started. Use
  this file to automatically start applications.

- The OS2INIT.CMD file runs every time an OS/2 screen group is started. Use it to set the **PATH**, **DPATH**, and other environment variables.
- The AUTOEXEC.BAT file runs when the DOS compatibility mode is first started.
- Use the CONFIG.SYS file to configure your system. Among other things, this file loads device drivers and specifies disk and multitasking parameters.
- Device drivers let you access hardware from OS/2.

11

Installing OS/2

With the introduction of OS/2, there are two primary operating systems for IBM personal computers and compatibles: DOS and OS/2. This chapter will explain how to set up OS/2 on your computer.

Note: You need to install OS/2 only once. After you have installed it on your hard disk, it is always there. When you turn on the computer, OS/2 will start.

Backing Up Your Programs and Data

If you are installing OS/2 on a computer that already has DOS data and programs on the hard disk, you may want to back up the files before installation. The IBM OS/2 version will not destroy any of your programs already on the hard disk; however, you should probably back up your disk anyway as a precautionary measure.

Installing OS/2: Maintaining DOS Bootability

If your computer already has DOS on it, you can boot DOS from a floppy if you decide to use it instead of OS/2. Thus, even though you have OS/2 installed on the hard disk, you can still use all of your programs that require DOS.

First, make a system floppy disk. Put a floppy in drive A and type:

```
FORMAT A: /S /V:BOOTDOS
```

After the floppy is formatted, copy the CONFIG.SYS and AUTOEXEC.BAT files to the floppy:

```
COPY C:\CONFIG.SYS A:
COPY C:\AUTOEXEC.BAT A:
```

If you do not already have a separate directory containing the DOS program commands, make a directory called DOS:

```
MD C:\DOS
```

Copy all DOS files, such as CHKDSK.COM and XCOPY.EXE to this directory. Also copy the CONFIG.SYS and AUTOEXEC.BAT files to this directory. Erase any DOS command files that you have stored in the root directory.

Next, edit all the device driver names in the CONFIG.SYS file on the A drive so that they contain the C: drive letter as well as the directory name. Also add:

```
SHELL=C:\DOS\COMMAND.COM
```

Now, edit the AUTOEXEC.BAT file on the A drive. Make the first line:

```
C:
```

and add:

```
SET COMSPEC=C:\DOS\COMMAND.COM
```

Make sure that any directories listed in **PATH** or **APPEND** commands also include a drive letter.

Once OS/2 is installed, you can boot DOS by first booting OS/2, then placing the DOS boot disk just discussed in the A drive and hitting Ctrl-Alt-Del. If you try to start DOS by putting the DOS disk in drive A and turning on the power, DOS might not be able to recognize the hard disk.

Installing OS/2

Put the *OS/2 installation disk* in drive A. Reboot the system by pressing *Ctrl-Alt-Del.* The computer will ask whether you want to do automatic or customized installation. Select automatic installation. Insert disk into drive A when prompted.

If you did not have DOS on your computer, the installation program will partition and format your hard disk. This could take it several minutes. If it asks you for partition size, set the whole disk as an OS/2 partition.

Summary

- To be safe, you may want to back up all of your files before installing OS/2 on a computer that already has DOS on it.
- You can boot DOS from an OS/2 computer by making a specially formatted DOS boot disk.
- Install OS/2 by putting the *OS/2 installation diskette* in drive A and pressing *Ctrl-Alt-Del.*

12

Utilities You Can Create

There are many powerful utilities you can create with batch files. This chapter contains some batch files that you may want to type in and use with your system. You can make any of these utilities with a text editor, such as a word processor, or by typing:

```
COPY CON: batch_name
```

If you use a word processor, be sure to save the programs in ASCII text form. You may want to put these files in a directory called BATCH or UTILITY and include the directory name in the **PATH** command.

Form Feeding Your Printer

This batch file, called FORMFEED, lets you automatically start a new page on your printer. You can use it when you are using Prt Sc, **COPY**, or **TYPE** to print files on your printer.

Type in the following program and call it FORMFEED.CMD.
Make a copy of it called FORMFEED.BAT.

```
ECHO OFF
REM This program form feeds the printer. It uses
 the file
REM called FF.
COPY FF PRN
```

Now, create a file called FF by:

```
COPY CON: FF
```

Hit Ctrl-L then Ctrl-Z. Put the file in the same directory as
FORMFEED.CMD.

Using FORMFEED

You plan to print two copies of a file called LOG.FIL. From the
OS/2 prompt you type:

```
COPY LOG.FIL PRN   (enter)
FORMFEED           (enter)
COPY LOG.FIL PRN (enter)
FORMFEED           (enter)
```

The two copies will be printed.

Making a Sorted List of All Subdirectories

The following program makes a sorted list of all subdirectories
in a group of directories. Type in the program and call it DIR-
LIST.CMD. Make a copy called DIRLIST.BAT.

```
ECHO OFF
REM This program makes a sorted list of all
 subdirectories
REM of a group of directories. You can pass it any
 number
REM of directories to go through.
REM
:DOTHESORT
REM List all files matching the file spec.
REM Extract all directory entries.
REM Sort the result.
ECHO ---Sorting the %1 directory---
DIR %1 | FIND "<DIR>" | SORT
ECHO --------------------------
REM
REM Now see if there are any more to sort.
REM
SHIFT
IF "%1" == "" GOTO END
GOTO :DOTHESORT
:END
REM All directories have been sorted.
```

Using DIRLIST

You want to make a sorted list of all directories in the root directory and the C:\LANGUAGE directory. You would:

```
DIRLIST \ C:\LANGUAGE
```

Now you want to make a sorted list of all directories in the root directory whose names start with OS:

```
DIRLIST \OS*.*
```

To send the results to a printer, you could:

```
DIRLIST \OS*.*  > PRN
FORMFEED
```

Making a Sorted List of All Files in Directories

The following program is similar to DIRLIST, only it lists all files as well as all directories. A sorted list of subdirectories is displayed before the sorted list of files. Type in the program and call it FILELIST.CMD. Make a copy called FILELIST.BAT.

```
@ ECHO OFF
REM This program makes a sorted list of all
  subdirectories
REM and files in a group of directories. The
  subdirectories
REM are displayed first. You can pass it any number
REM of directories to go through.
REM
:DOTHESORT
ECHO ---Sorting %1---
REM List all subdirectories matching the file spec.
DIR %1 | FIND "<DIR>" | SORT
REM
REM Now sort the other files.
REM
DIR %1 | FIND /V "<DIR>" | FIND /V "Volume" | FIND
  /V "Directory" | FIND /V "File(s)" | SORT
ECHO ----------------
REM
REM Now see if there are any more to sort.
REM
SHIFT
IF "%1" == "" GOTO END
GOTO DOTHESORT
:END
REM All directories have been sorted.
```

Using FILELIST

You want to make a sorted list of all files and directories in the C:\, C:\OS2SYS, and C:\OS2 directories. You could:

```
FILELIST C:\ C:\OS2SYS C:\OS2
```

Now you want a sorted list of all device drivers in the OS2SYS directory. You could:

```
FILELIST C:\OS2SYS\*.SYS
```

Searching for Text within a Group of Files

This next utility lets you look for a specific phrase within a group of files. For example, you can search for all occurrences of the line "Oscar the Grouch." The phrase can contain any number of words. However, there cannot be more than one space between each of the words. The file to search through is the first parameter passed to FINDTEXT. It can contain wild cards.

Type the program into a file called FINDTEXT.CMD. Copy the file to FINDTEXT.BAT. Note the use of the environment for temporarily storing variables.

```
@ ECHO OFF
REM This program searches a group of files
REM for specific text. The text can contain any
REM number of words.
REM
REM At least two parameters must be given.
IF "%2" == "" GOTO ERROR
REM Set the file name (pattern) to search.
SET ftfnm=%1
REM Set the search string.
SET ftstr=%2
SHIFT
```

```
REM
REM As long as there are more words in the phrase, add
REM them to the search string.
:CREATESRCH
SHIFT
IF "%1" == "" GOTO FINDIT
SET ftstr=%ftstr% %1
GOTO CREATESRCHREM
REM Now search through all matching files for the
 text.
:FINDIT
FOR %%a IN (%ftfnm%) DO FIND "%ftstr%" %%a
REM
REM Now clear out the environment variables.
SET ftstr=
SET ftfnm=
GOTO END
REM
REM The user didn't give enough parameters.
:ERROR
ECHO Not enough parameters entered.
:END
```

Using FINDTEXT

Suppose you want to find all letters in the BUSINESS\LET-TERS directory that contain the name Daniel Bakal. You could:

```
FINDTEXT BUSINESS\LETTERS\*.* Daniel Bakal
```

Changing the Date on a Group of Files

The following program updates the file date on a group of files. This lets you make all programs on a disk have the same date and time stamp. Programmers can use this to force recompilation of all files. You can also use it to force backups of a group of files or to give an orderly appearance to a disk that you are marketing.

Type this program in and call it TOUCH.CMD. Make a copy called TOUCH.BAT.

```
@ ECHO OFF
REM This program updates the file date and time
REM of a group of files.
REM
:DOUPDATE
COPY %1 + /B
REM Now see if there are more
SHIFT
IF "%1" == "" GOTO END
GOTO DOUPDATE
:END
REM Finished.
```

Using TOUCH

You are sending a disk containing a bunch of drawings you have made to a friend. You want all of the files to have the same time and date. You could:

```
TOUCH A:*.*
```

You are writing a program composed of several modules. To make sure that all modules are recompiled, you could:

```
TOUCH *.C
```

Printing a System Use Log

Every time that you reboot the computer, the following program will display the last time you started working. This is useful for remembering the last time that you used the system. You could expand this program to make a more complicated log-on procedure, perhaps requiring a password.

Start by making a file called CR. Enter:

```
COPY CON: CR
```

Then hit Return and Ctrl-Z.

Next, type in the following program called LASTLOG.CMD:

```
@ ECHO OFF
REM This program displays a message indicating the
 last
REM time the system was used.
REM The time last used is kept in a file called
REM LASTLOG.FIL.
IF NOT EXIST LASTLOG.FIL GOTO UPDATELOG
ECHO --------------------------------
ECHO Last log on was:
TYPE LASTLOG.FIL
ECHO --------------------------------
DEL LASTLOG.FIL
PAUSE
:UPDATELOG
REM Put in the current date and time.
DATE < CR > LASTLOG.FIL
TIME < CR >> LASTLOG.FIL
REM Finished.
```

Next, put the following line in the STARTUP.CMD file:

```
LASTLOG
```

If you do not already have a STARTUP.CMD file, you can use the following:

```
LASTLOG
EXIT
```

Summary

- FORMFEED starts a new page on the printer.
- DIRLIST creates a sorted list of all subdirectories within a group of directories.
- FILELIST creates a sorted list of all files and subdirectories within a group of directories. The subdirectories are listed first.
- FINDTEXT searches a group of files for a text phrase.
- TOUCH updates the file date and time on a group of files.
- LASTLOG displays the last date and time the system was used every time that you boot OS/2.

Appendix A
Summary of Using OS/2

Installing OS/2

Place the OS/2 installation disk in the A drive. Turn on the computer. Follow the instructions. The program will automatically set up OS/2 and all the necessary system files.

Starting OS/2

Once OS/2 is installed, you need only turn on the computer for OS/2 to start.

Running Programs

If you are not in the Session Manager, hit Ctrl-Esc. The Session Manager will appear. On the left is a list of programs you can start; on the right is a list of programs currently running. To start a new program, move the cursor to a program in the left column and hit Return. To switch to a running program, move the cursor to a program in the right column and hit Return.

If you want to run a program that is not listed in the Session Manager, move the cursor to the OS/2 command prompt in the left column and hit Return. An OS/2 prompt will appear on the screen. Type in the name of the program that you want to run. If there is an error message, make sure that you spelled the name of the program properly. If you did, use the CHDIR command to switch to the directory containing the program. Enter the program name again.

Running DOS Programs

If you need to run a program not designed for OS/2, call up the Session Manager, move the cursor to the DOS command prompt entry (in the right column) and hit Enter. This will start the DOS compatibility mode. Run the program.

Going to the Session Manager

Hitting Ctrl-Esc puts you in the Session Manager.

Switching between Screen Groups

To switch between running programs, hit Alt-Esc.

Leaving OS/2

If there are any programs running, switch to them and exit them. This will insure that any temporary files they are using are cleaned up. Then turn off the computer.

Booting DOS

If you need to run programs built only for the DOS environment and they won't run in the DOS compatibility mode, you should boot DOS. First start OS/2. Then put a DOS system disk in the A drive (Chapter 11 tells you how to make one). Hit Ctrl-Alt-Del. DOS will start.

Some Common Directory Operations

Most application programs will have menus built in to help you load and save files. These menus will also let you move through the disk directory structure. If for some reason you need to work with files outside of an application program, you will find the following commands useful. These commands must be entered from the OS/2 or DOS compatibility mode prompt.

Seeing What Files Are on the Disk

Use the **DIR** command to see what files are on the disk. If you type **DIR** without parameters, all files and directories in the current directory will be listed. You can also instruct **DIR** to look at files in a different drive or directory or to list only certain files. For example, you want to see what files are on the disk. Enter:

```
DIR
```

If you want a printout of the list, type:

```
DIR > PRN
```

Making a List of All Files on a Disk

Use the **TREE** command to make a list of all files on a disk. It will print out all the directories and all the files within the directories. You must give it the name of the drive containing the disk. For example, you are not sure where a particular file on your hard disk is located. To find out, enter:

```
TREE C: /F
```

To get a printout of the list, type:

```
TREE C: /F > PRN
```

Changing to a Different Disk Drive

The first letter in the prompt indicates the current disk drive. For example, [C:\] means the current drive is the C drive. To switch to a different drive, type the name of the drive, followed by a colon, then hit Enter. For example, you are currently in the C drive, but want to switch to the A drive. Enter:

```
A:
```

To return to the C drive, enter:

```
C:
```

Switching Directories

The prompt also indicates the current directory. For example, [C:\] means you are in the root directory. [C:\WORDPROC] means that you are in the word processor directory. Use the **CHDIR** command to switch directories. If the directory you want to switch to is a subdirectory of the directory you are in, just enter **CHDIR** followed by the name of the directory. If you want to switch to the parent of the directory you are in, enter **CHDIR....** If you want to switch to any other directory, you must type in its full name, starting from the root directory. For example, you are in the root directory and want to switch to the WORDPROC directory. The WORDPROC directory is a subdirectory of the root directory. Enter:

```
CHDIR WORDPROC
```

Now you want to switch back to the parent directory. Enter:

```
CHDIR ..
```

You want to switch to the \LETTERS\TAYLOR directory. Enter:

```
CHDIR \LETTERS\TAYLOR
```

You can always return to the root directory by entering:

```
CHDIR \
```

File Maintenance Routines

The following group of commands is useful for file maintenance. As with the directory operations, most application software will have routines to help you with file maintenance.

Copying Files

You may need to copy files to a floppy disk for backup purposes or so that you can use the files on a different computer. You may also need to copy files when installing new software. Use the **XCOPY** command. Give it the location and name of the source file and the location in which the copy should be placed. You can use ***.*** to indicate all files from the source directory. If you end the command with **/S**, all files in subdirectories will be copied as well. For example, you want to copy the file BLUEBERR.PM to the disk in the A drive. Enter:

```
XCOPY BLUEBERR.PM A:
```

You want to copy all files in the INVOICES directory to the D drive. Enter:

```
XCOPY INVOICES D:
```

You just got a new application disk and want to copy all the files to the NEWAPP directory. Enter:

```
XCOPY A:*.* NEWAPP /S
```

Erasing Files

Use the **DEL** command to erase files. Enter **DEL** followed by the name of the file. (You can also use the **ERASE** command; they are exactly the same.) For example, you want to erase the file MUD.MP. Enter:

```
DEL MUD.MP
```

Creating New Directories

You can create a new directory with the **MKDIR** command. Follow it by the name of the new directory. The directory will be made within the directory you are in. You can put the new directory within any directory by giving its full path name. For example, you want to make a directory called REALIZER. Enter:

```
MKDIR REALIZER
```

You want to make a directory called GWPHAM. You want it to be located in the root directory. Enter:

```
MKDIR \GWPHAM
```

Backups

When you get new software on a floppy disk, you should make a backup copy of it. If by some accident the original is destroyed, you can use the backup. Do this before you install the software on your hard disk. First put or set write protect tabs on the original disks. Then, enter:

```
DISKCOPY A: A:
```

When OS/2 asks for the source disk, put in the first original disk. When OS/2 asks for the target disk, put in a blank disk.

You may need to switch the disks in and out several times. When the program is finished, the blank disk will contain a complete copy of the original. Label it. If the application contains several disks, repeat the procedure for each one. This will give you a complete backup set. Put the originals in a safe place. Use the backups for installing the software on your hard disk.

You should also make frequent backups of your hard disk. Thus, if your hard disk has a problem, you will have a backup of your programs and data. Use the **BACKUP** command, commercial backup software, or a hardware backup system.

Preparing Disks for Use

If you plan to copy files to a floppy disk, the disk must be formatted. Since formatting destroys all data that is already on a disk, format all disks when you get a new box. Put a blank label on them so that you know they are already formatted.

To format a disk, put a blank disk in the A drive and type:

```
FORMAT A:
```

Advanced Features

There are several things advanced users can do to customize their system. This section briefly outlines these. Refer to Chapters 6 through 10 for details.

If you want certain programs to automatically start when you turn on the computer, create or edit the STARTUP.CMD file. Use the **START** command to start the programs. If you put the **EXIT** command at the end of the STARTUP.CMD file, OS/2 will automatically start the Session Manager after it starts the other applications.

Use the **PATH** command so that OS/2 can automatically find where your application programs are located. Put the **PATH** command in the OS2INIT.CMD file.

The installation program will automatically set up the CON-FIG.SYS file for the hardware that you have. You can edit the CONFIG.SYS file to tailor your system's performance. As you add new hardware, you may want to change the CONFIG.SYS settings. You can also add a RAM disk by adding the VDISK.SYS driver to the CONFIG.SYS file.

Appendix B
OS/2 and DOS
Command Differences

The following table summarizes the differences between the OS/2 and DOS commands. It indicates whether each command works in OS/2 mode and DOS compatibility mode, whether an analogous command existed in DOS, and if there are significant changes in the format or usage of the command between DOS and OS/2. It also indicates if the command has been enhanced to take multiple parameters. For example, in DOS, **DEL** takes one file name as a parameter; in OS/2 it takes several. The table also includes the batch file and configuration file commands.

Commands

Command	OS/2 Mode	Compatibility Mode	DOS	Multiple Parameter Extension	Signigicant Changes
ANSI	*				*
APPEND		*	*		
ASSIGN		*	*		Avoid Use
ATTRIB	*	*	*		
BACKUP	*	*	*		*
BREAK		*	*		
CHCP	*	*	*		
CHDIR	*	*	*		
CHKDSK	*	*	*		*
CLS	*	*	*		
CMD	*				*

Command	OS/2 Mode	Compatibility Mode	DOS	Multiple Parameter Extension	Signigicant Changes
COMMAND		*	*		
COMP	*	*	*		*
COPY	*	*	*		
DATE	*	*	*		
DEL	*	*	*	*	
DETACH	*				*
DIR	*	*	*	*	
DISKCOMP	*	*	*		
DISKCOPY	*	*	*		
DPATH	*				*
ERASE	*	*	*	*	
EXIT	*	*	*		
FDISK	*	*	*		*
FIND	*	*	*		
FORMAT	*	*	*		
GRAFTABL		*	*		
HELP	*	*			*
HELPMSG	*	*			*
JOIN		*	*		
KEYB	*	*	*		*
LABEL	*	*	*		
MKDIR	*	*	*	*	
MODE	*	*	*		*
MORE	*	*	*		
PATCH	*	*			*
PATH	*	*	*		
PRINT	*	*	*		*
PROMPT	*	*	*		
RECOVER	*	*	*		
RENAME	*	*	*		
REPLACE	*	*	*		
RESTORE	*	*	*		*
RMDIR	*	*	*	*	
SET	*	*	*		
SETCOM40		*			*

Command	OS/2 Mode	Compatibility Mode	DOS	Multiple Parameter Extension	Signigicant Changes
SORT	*	*	*		
SPOOL	*	*			*
START	*				*
SUBST		*	*		
SYS	*	*	*		
TIME	*	*	*		
TREE	*	*	*		
TYPE	*	*	*	*	
VER	*	*	*		
VERIFY	*	*	*		
VOL	*	*	*	*	
XCOPY	*	*	*		
	*	*	*		
>n	*	*			*
>>	*	*	*		
<	*	*	*		
|	*	*	*		
&	*	*			*
&&	*	*			*
||	*	*			*
( )	*	*			*

Batch Commands

Command	OS/2 Mode	Compatibility Mode	DOS	Multiple Parameter Extension	Signigicant Changes
CALL	*	*	*		
ECHO	*	*	*		
ENDLOCAL	*	*			*
EXTPROC	*	*			*
FOR	*	*	*		

Command	OS/2 Mode	Compatibility Mode	DOS	Multiple Parameter Extension	Significant Changes
GOTO	*	*	*		
IF	*	*	*		
PAUSE	*	*	*		*
REM	*	*	*		
SETLOCAL	*	*			*
SHIFT	*	*	*		

Configuration Commands

Command	OS/2 Mode	Compatibility Mode	DOS	Multiple Parameter Extension	Signigicant Changes
BREAK	*		*		
BUFFERS	*		*		
CODEPAGE	*		*		
COUNTRY	*		*		
DEVICE	*		*		
DEVINFO	*				*
DISKCACHE	*				*
FCBS	*		*		
IOPL	*				*
LIBPATH	*				*
MAXWAIT	*				*
MEMMAN	*				*
PRIORITY	*				*
PROTECTONLY		*			*
PROTSHELL	*				*
RMSIZE	*				*
RUN	*				*
REM	*				*
SHELL	*		*		
SWAPPATH	*				*
THREADS	*				*
TIMESLICE	*				*

Device Drivers

Command	OS/2 Mode	Compatibility Mode	DOS	Multiple Parameter Extension	Signigicant Changes
ANSI.SYS		*	*		
COM.SYS	*	*			*
EGA.SYS	*	*			*
EXTDSKDD.SYS	*	*	*	*	
MOUSE.SYS	*	*	*		*
POINTDD.SYS	*	*			*
VDISK.SYS	*	*	*		

Key Combinations

Command	OS/2 Mode	Compatibility Mode	DOS	Multiple Parameter Extension	Signigicant Changes
Alt – Esc	*	*			*
Ctrl – Alt – Delete	*	*	*		
Ctrl – Alt – PrtSc		*			*
Ctrl – C	*	*	*		
Ctrl – Esc	*	*			*
Ctrl – PrtSc	*	*	*		
PrtSc	*	*	*		

Appendix C
Quick Summary
of Commands

ANSI

Format:

This command allows programs to use the ANSI escape sequences for character control.

ANSI [(ON) (OFF)]

APPEND

Format:

This function sets a path where DOS programs will look for data files.

APPEND [[*drive:*] *path*] [;[*drive*]*path*] [...] [/E]

ASSIGN

Format:

This function lets you use a different drive letter name for a disk drive.

ASSIGN [*actual_drive_name* = *new_drive_name*] [...]

ATTRIB

Format:

This command changes the read-only or archive attribute of a file.

ATTRIB [(+) (-) R] [(+) (-) A] [*drive_name:*] [*path_name*] *file_name* [/S]

BACKUP

Format:

Backs up files from one disk to another.

BACKUP [*source_drive:*][*source_path*][*source_filename*] [*destination_drive:*] [/S] [/M] [/A] [/F] [/D:*date*] [/T:*time*] [/L:*log_file_name*]

BREAK

Format:

This command enables or disables Control-C and Control-Break checking after OS/2 commands.

BREAK [(ON) (OFF)]

CHCP   This function selects or displays the code
                        page.
Format: CHCP [*code_page_number*]

CHDIR or **CD**   This command changes or displays the
                        default (current working) directory.
Format: CHDIR [[*drive_name:*]*path_name*]
                        CD [[*drive_name:*]*path_name*]

CHKDSK   This function checks disk usage and reports
                        any disk errors.
Format: CHKDSK [*drive_name:*]
                        [[*path_name*]*file_name*] [/F] [/V]

CLS   This command clears the display screen.
Format: CLS

CMD   This function starts a secondary command
                        processor in the OS/2 Protected Mode.
Format: CMD [*drive_name:*][*path_name*] [(/C *string*)
                        (/K *string*)]

COMMAND   This function starts a secondary command
                        processor in the DOS Compatibility Mode.
Format: COMMAND [*drive_name:*][*path_name*] [(/P)
                        (/C *string*)] [/E:*environment_size*]

COMP   This command compares the contents of one
                        group of files with the contents of another
                        group of files.
Format: COMP [*group1_drive_name*]
                        [*group1_path_name*] [*group1_file_name*]
                        [*group2_drive_name*] [*group2_path_name*]
                        [*group2_file_name*]

COPY   This command copies a file or group of files.
Format: COPY [*source_drive_name:*]
                        [*source_path_name*] [*source_file_name*]

[(/A) (/B)] [*dest_drive_name:*]
[*dest_path_name*] [*dest_file_name*]
[(/A) (/B)] [/V]

COPY [*source1_drive_name:*]
  [*source1_path_name*] [*source1_file_name*]
  [(/A) (/B)] + [*source2_drive_name:*]
  [*source2_path_name*] [*source2_file_name*]
  [(/A) (/B)] [+ ...] [*dest_drive_name:*]
  [*dest_path_name*] [*dest_file_name*] [(/A)
  (/B)] [/V]

DATE	This command sets or checks the date.
Format:	DATE [*mm-dd-yy*]
DEL	Erase a file or group of files.
Format:	DEL [[*drive_name:*] [*path_name*] [*file_name*]] [...]
DETACH	This function causes a program to run in the background.
Format:	DETACH *program_name* [*arguments*]
DIR	This commands lists all the files and directories within a directory.
Format:	DIR [[*drive_name:*] [*path_name*] [*file_name*]] [...] [/P] [/W]
DISKCOMP	This command compares, byte for byte, two floppy disks.
Format:	DISKCOMP [*first_drive*] [*second_drive*]
DISKCOPY	This command copies, byte for byte, one floppy to another.
Format:	DISKCOPY [*source_drive_name:*] [*target_drive_name:*]

DPATH

This function sets a path where OS/2 programs will look for data files.

Format: DPATH [[*drive:*] *path*] [;[*drive*]*path*] [...]

ERASE

This command erases a file or group of files.

Format: ERASE [[*drive_name:*] [*path_name*]
          [*file_name*]] [...]

EXIT

This command leaves a screen group.

Format: EXIT

FDISK

This command switches the active partition, or reconfigures the partition structure of the hard disk.

Format: FDISK

FIND

This command searches a file or a group of files for the specified text.

Format: FIND [/V] [(/C) (/N)] "*text*" [[*drive_name:*]
          [*path_name*] [*file_name*]] [...]

FORMAT

This command prepares a new disk for use.

Format: FORMAT [*drive:*] [/4] [/T:*tracks_per_disk*]
          [/N:*sectors_per_track*] [/S] [/V[:*label*]]

GRAFTABL

Loads a table of extended characters to be used on graphics screens.

Format: GRAFTABL [(*code_page*) (?) (/STA)]

HELP

This command explains the meaning of OS/2 error messages.

Format: HELP [(ON) (OFF) (*message_number*)]

HELPMSG

This command explains the meaning of OS/2 error messages.

Format: HELPMSG *message_number*

JOIN   This command substitutes a drive for a directory name.
Format: JOIN [*drive_to_use*: *drive*:*directory_
                         to_disable*]
                       JOIN *joined_drive_to_cancel*: /D

KEYBxx   This command replaces the US keyboard
                       layout with a different country's keyboard.
Format: KEYB*xx*

LABEL   This function creates or changes a disk's
                       volume label.
Format: LABEL [*drive_name*:][*label_text*]

MKDIR or **MD**   This command creates a new directory.
Format: MKDIR [[*drive_name*:][*path_name*][*new_
                         directory_name*]] [...]

MODE   This command lets you initialize parallel port,
                       serial port, and display characteristics.
Format: MODE *display_mode* [, *number_of_lines*]

                       MODE LPT*number* [*characters_per_line*] [,
                         [*lines_per_inch*][,P]]

                       MODE COM*number*:*baud* [, *parity* [,*databits*
                         [,*stopbits*]]] [,TO = (ON) (OFF)] [,XON =
                         (ON) (OFF)] [,IDSR = (ON) (OFF)]
                         [,ODSR = (ON) (OFF)] [,OCTS = (ON)
                         (OFF)] [,DTR = (ON) (OFF)] [,RTS =
                         (ON) (OFF)]

                       MODE COM*number*[:] *baud* [,*parity*
                         [,*databits* [, *stopbits*] [,P]]]
                       MODE COM*number*

MORE   This command pauses an output listing every
                         time the screen is filled.

Format: MORE < *source_file*
                          source_program | MORE

PATCH   This command modifies particular bytes of a
                         program file.

Format: PATCH [[*drive_name:*] [*path_name*]
                          file_name] [/A]

PATH   This function defines a group of directories to
                         search for programs not found in the current
                         directory.

Format: PATH [[*drive_name:*][*path_name*]] [; ...]

PRINT   This command prints a file or series of files.
                         You can continue to work while the files are
                         printing.

Format: PRINT [/D:*printer_to_use*] [/B] [
                          [*drive_name:*] [*path_name*] [*file_name*]]
                          [...]
                         PRINT [/D:*printer_to_use*] [(/C) (/T)]

PROMPT   This command sets the style of the system
                         prompt.

Format: PROMPT [*text*]

RECOVER   This function files from a damaged disk.
Format: RECOVER [*drive_name:*] [*path_name*]
                          file_name
                          RECOVER *drive_name*

RENAME or **REN** This command renames a file or group of
                         files.

Format: RENAME [*drive_name:*] [*directory_name*]
                          original_name new_name
                         REN [*drive_name:*] [*directory_name*]
                          original_name new_name

REPLACE

This command lets you replace files in one directory with files of the same name from another directory.

Format:

REPLACE [*source_drive:*] [*source_path*] [*source_file*] [*target_drive:*] [*target_path*] [(/S) (/A)] [/P] [/R] [/W]

RESTORE

This command lets you restore files to a disk from a backup disk.

Format:

RESTORE *back_up_drive:* [*target_drive*] [*target_path*] [*target_file*] [/S] [/P] [/B:*date*] [/A: *date*] [/E: *time*] [/L: *time*] [/M] [/N]

RMDIR or **RD**

This command removes a directory structure or group of directory structures.

Format:

RMDIR [[*drive:*] [*path*]] [...] RD [[*drive:*] [*path*]] [...]

SET

This command equates a value to a variable in the environment.

Format:

SET [*var_name* = [*var_value*]]

SETCOM40

This command allows DOS programs that use a modem, serial printer, plotter, or mouse to operate in the DOS Compatibility Mode.

Format:

SETCOM40 COM*number* = (ON) (OFF)

SORT

This command sorts a file.

Format:

program | SORT [/R] [/+*start_col*] SORT [/R] [/+*start_col*] *file_name*

SPOOL

This command allows application print outs to be spooled, by setting up a print buffer.

Format:

SPOOL [*drive_name:*] [*directory_name*] [/D:*device*] [/O: *device*]

START

This command starts a new OS/2 screen group and runs a program in it.

Format:

START ["*program_title*"] [/C] *program_name* [*program_parameters*]

SUBST

This command substitutes a drive name for a path.

Format:

SUBST [*new_drive*: *real_drive*:*real_directory*] SUBST *drive*:[*directory*] /D

SYS

This command creates an OS/2 system disk by copying the OS/2 system files.

Format:

SYS *drive*:

TIME

This command sets or changes the system time.

Format:

TIME [*hours*:*minutes*[:*seconds*[.*hundredths*]]]

TREE

This command displays the directory structure of the disk.

Format:

TREE [*drive*:] [/F]

TYPE

This command types out a file or files.

Format:

TYPE [[*drive_name*:] [*directory_name*][*file_name*]] [...]

VER

This command displays the OS/2 version number.

Format:

VER

VERIFY

This command selects the verify status.

Format:

VERIFY [(ON) (OFF)]

VOL

This command prints a disk's volume label.

Format:

VOL [*drive_name*:] [...]

XCOPY

This command is an extended file copier.

Format: XCOPY [*source_drive:*] [*source_path*]
                 [*source_file*] [*dest_drive:*] [*dest_path*]
                 [*dest_file*] [/S [/ E]] [/P] [/V] [(/A)
                 (/M)] [/D:*date*]

Appendix D
Command Groups

This appendix breaks the OS/2 commands into related groups.

File Management Commands

ATTRIB This command changes the read-only or archive attribute of a file.

Format: ATTRIB [(+) (-) R] [(+) (-) A] [*drive_name:*] [*path_name*] *file_name* [/S]

COMP This command compares the contents of one group of files with the contents of another group of files.

Format: COMP [*group1_drive_name*] [*group1_path_name*] [*group1_file_name*] [*group2_drive_name*] [*group2_path_name*] [*group2_file_name*]

COPY This command copies a file or group of files.

Format: COPY [*source_drive_name:*] [*source_path_name*] [*source_file_name*] [(/A) (/B)][*dest_drive_name:*] [*dest_path_name*] [*dest_file_name*] [(/A) (/B)][/V]
COPY [*source1_drive_name:*] [*source1_path_name*] [*source1_file_name*] [(/A) (/B)]+[*source2_drive_name:*] [*source2_path_name*] [*source2_file_name*] [(/A) (/B)] [+ ...][*dest_drive_name:*]

[dest_path_name] [dest_file_name] [(/A)
(/B)][/V]

DEL   Erase a file or group of files.
Format: DEL [[drive_name:] [path_name] [file_name]
                 ][...]

DIR   This commands lists all the files and direc-
                 tories within a directory.
Format: DIR [[drive_name:] [path_name] [file_name]
                 ][...][/P] [/W]

ERASE   This command erases a file or group of files.
Format: ERASE [[drive_name:] [path_name]
                 [file_name]][...]

RECOVER   This function files from a damaged disk.
Format: RECOVER [drive_name:] [path_name]
                 file_name
                 RECOVER drive_name

RENAME or **REN** This command renames a file or group of
                 files.
Format: RENAME [drive_name:] [directory_name]
                 original_name new_name
                 REN [drive_name:] [directory_name]
                 original_name new_name

REPLACE   This command lets you replace files in one
                 directory with files of the same name from
                 another directory.
Format: REPLACE [source_drive:] [source_path]
                 [source_file][target_drive:] [target_path]
                 [(/S) (/A)][/P][/R][/W]

VERIFY	This command selects the verify status.
Format:	VERIFY [(ON) (OFF)]
XCOPY	This command is an extended file copier.
Format:	XCOPY [*source_drive:*] [*source_path*]
	[*source_file*][*dest_drive:*] [*dest_path*]
	[*dest_file*][/S [/ E]][/P][/V][(/A)
	(/M)][/D:*date*]

Directory Management Commands

CHDIRorCD	This command changes or displays the default (current working) directory.
Format:	CHDIR [[*drive_name:*]*path_name*]
	CD[[*drive_name:*]*path_name*]
DIR	This commands lists all the files and directories within a directory.
Format:	DIR [[*drive_name:*] [*path_name*] [*file_name*]][...][/P] [/W]
MKDIR or **MD**	This command creates a new directory.
Format:	MKDIR [[*drive_name:*][*path_name*][*new_directory_name*]] [...]
RMDIRorRD	This command removes a directory structure or group of directory structures.
Format:	RMDIR[[*drive:*] [*path*]][...]
	RD[[*drive:*] [*path*]][...]
TREE	This command displays the directory structure of the disk.
Format:	TREE[*drive:*][/F]

Disk Management Commands

BACKUP
Format:
	Backs up files from one disk to another.
	BACKUP
	[*source_drive:*][*source_path*][*source_filename*]
	  [*destination_drive:*] [/S] [/M] [/A] [/F]
	  [/D:*date*] [/T:*time*] [/L:*log_file_name*]

CHKDSK Format:	This function checks disk usage and reports any disk errors. CHKDSK [*drive_name:*] [[*path_name*][*file_name*] [/F] [/V]
DISKCOMP Format:	This command compares, byte for byte, two floppy disks. DISKCOMP [*first_drive*] [*second_drive*]
DISKCOPY Format:	This command copies, byte for byte, one floppy to another. DISKCOPY [*source_drive_name:*] [*target_drive_name:*]
FORMAT Format:	This command prepares a new disk for use. FORMAT [*drive:*] [/4] [/T:*tracks_per_disk*] [/N:*sectors_per_track*] [/S] [/V[:*label*]]
LABEL Format:	This function creates or changes a disk's volume label. LABEL [*drive_name:*][*label_text*]

RESTORE
 	
Format:
	This command lets you restore files to a disk from a backup disk.
	RESTORE *back_up_drive:* [*target_drive*]
	  [*target_path*] [*target_file*][/S][/P][/B: *date*] [/A: *date*][/E: *time*][/L: *time*
	  [[/M][/N]

SYS	This command creates an OS/2 system disk by copying the OS/2 system files.
Format:	SYS *drive*:
VOL	This command prints a disk's volume label.
Format:	VOL [*drive_name*:] [...]

Environment Commands

APPEND	This function sets a path where DOS programs will look for data files.
Format:	APPEND [[*drive*:] *path*] [;[*drive*]*path*] [...][/E]
ASSIGN	This function lets you use a different drive letter name for a disk drive.
Format:	ASSIGN [*actual_drive_name* = *new_drive_name*] [...]
DPATH	This function sets a path where OS/2 programs will look for data files.
Format:	DPATH[[*drive*:] *path*] [;[*drive*]*path*] [...]
JOIN	This command substitutes a drive for a directory name.
Format:	JOIN [*drive_to_use*:*drive*:*directory_to_disable*] JOIN *joined_drive_to_cancel*: /D
PATH	This function defines a group of directories to search for programs not found in the current directory.
Format:	PATH [[*drive_name*:][*path_name*]] [; ...]
PROMPT	This command sets the style of the system prompt.
Format:	PROMPT [*text*]

SET	This command equates a value to a variable in the environment.
Format:	SET [*var_name* = [*var_value*]]
SUBST	This command substitutes a drive name for a path.
Format:	SUBST[*new_drive:real_drive:real_directory*] SUBST*drive:*[*directory*] /D

Device Commands

ANSI	This command allows programs to use the ANSI escape sequences for character control.
Format:	ANSI [(ON) (OFF)]
CHCP	This function selects or displays the code page.
Format:	CHCP [*code_page_number*]
CLS	This command clears the display screen.
Format:	CLS
FDISK	This command switches the active partition, or reconfigures the partition structure of the hard disk.
Format:	FDISK
GRAFTABL	Loads a table of extended characters to be used on graphics screens.
Format:	GRAFTABL[(*code_page*) (?) (/STA)]
KEYBxx	This command replaces the US keyboard layout with a different country's keyboard.
Format:	KEYB*xx*

MODE   This command lets you initialize parallel port,
                    serial port, and display characteristics.
Format: MODE *display_mode* [, *number_of_lines*]
                      MODE LPT*number* [*characters_per_line*]
                      [, [*lines_per_inch*][,P]]
                      MODE COM*number*:*baud* [, *parity*
                      [,*databits* [,*stopbits*]]] [,TO = (ON) (OFF)
                      ][,XON = (ON) (OFF)][,IDSR = (ON)
                      (OFF)][,ODSR = (ON) (OFF)][,OCTS =
                      (ON) (OFF)][,DTR = (ON) (OFF)]
                      [,RTS = (ON) (OFF)]
                      MODE COM*number*[:] *baud* [,*parity*
                      [,*databits* [, *stopbits*] [,P]]]
                    MODE COM*number*

SETCOM40   This command allows DOS programs that use
                    a modem, serial printer, plotter, or mouse to
                    operate in the DOS Compatibility Mode.
Format: SETCOM40 COM*number* = (ON) (OFF)

Output Commands

PRINT   This command prints a file or series of
                    files.You can continue to work while the files
                    are printing.
Format: PRINT [/D:*printer_to_use*] [/B]
                      [[*drive_name*:] [*path_name*] [*file_name*]]
                      [...]
                    PRINT [/D:*printer_to_use*][(/C) (/T)]

SPOOL   This command allows application print outs
                    to be spooled, by setting up a print buffer.
Format: SPOOL [*drive_name*:] [*directory_name*]
                      [/D:*device*] [/O: *device*]

TYPE	This command types out a file or files.
Format:	TYPE[[*drive_name:*][*direc-tory_name*][*file_name*]][...]

Filters

FIND	This command searches a file or a group of files for the specified text.
Format:	FIND [/V][(/C) (/N)]"*text*"[[*drive_name:*] [*path_name*] [*file_name*]][...]
MORE	This command pauses an output listing every time the screen is filled.
Format:	MORE*source_file* *source_program* I MORE
SORT	This command sorts a file.
Format:	*program* I SORT [/R] [/+*start_col*] SORT [/R] [/+*start_col*]*file_name*

Miscellaneous

BREAK	This command enables or disables Control-C and Control-Break checking after OS/2 commands.
Format:	BREAK [(ON) (OFF)]
CMD	This function starts a secondary command processor in the OS/2 Protected Mode.
Format:	CMD [*drive_name:*][*path_name*] [(/C *string*) (/K *string*)]
COMMAND	This function starts a secondary command processor in the DOS Compatibility Mode.

Format:	COMMAND [*drive_name:*][*path_name*] [(/P) (/C *string*)] [/E:*environment_size*]
DATE	This command sets or checks the date.
Format:	DATE [*mm-dd-yy*]
DETACH	This function causes a program to run in the background.
Format:	DETACH *program_name* [*arguments*]
EXIT	This command leaves a screen group.
Format:	EXIT
HELP	This command explains the meaning of OS/2 error messages.
Format:	HELP [(ON) (OFF) (*message_number*)]
HELPMSG	This command explains the meaning of OS/2 error messages.
Format:	HELPMSG *message_number*
PATCH	This command modifies particular bytes of a program file.
Format:	PATCH [[*drive_name:*] [*path_name*] *file_name*] [/A]
START	This command starts a new OS/2 screen group and runs a program in it.
Format:	START ["*program_title*"] [/C] *program_name* [*program_parameters*]
TIME	This command sets or changes the system time.
Format:	TIME[*hours:minutes*[*:seconds*[*.hundredths*]]]
VER	This command displays the OS/2 version number.
Format:	VER

Bibliography

Microsoft OS/2 Toolkit
IBM OS/2 Toolkit
Microsoft DOS 3.2 Reference Manual
Microsoft C Compiler Run-Time Library Reference Manual

Index

Also Available in Bantam's PC Library

PC Configuration Handbook by John Woram

Lance Leventhal's 80386 Programming Guide by
Lance Leventhal

Executive Guide to PC Presentation Graphics by
Gordon McComb

*Power Computing: Multitasking and Application Management
with Your 80386* by Winn L. Rosch